W9-BTF-258

WOVEN LEADERSHIP

David,
Lead with
Diversity!

WOVEN
LEADERSHIP

THE POWER OF DIVERSITY
TO TRANSFORM YOUR
ORGANIZATION FOR SUCCESS

KIM BOX

Copyright © 2011 by Kim Box. All rights reserved.

No part of this publication may be reproduced, stored in a retrieval system, or transmitted in any form or by any means, electronic, mechanical, photocopying, recording, scanning, or otherwise, without the prior written permission of the author.

Limit of Liability/Disclaimer of Warranty: While the publisher and author have used their best efforts in preparing this book, they make no representations or warranties with respect to the accuracy or completeness of the contents of this book and specifically disclaim any implied warranties of merchantability or fitness for a particular purpose. No warranty may be created or extended by sales representatives or written sales materials. The advice and strategies contained herein may not be suitable for your situation. You should consult with a professional when appropriate. Neither the publisher nor the author shall be liable for any loss of profit or any other commercial damages, including but not limited to special, incidental, consequential, personal, or other damages.

Woven Leadership: The Power of Diversity to Transform Your Organization for Success
By Kim Box
1. Business & Economics : Leadership 2. Business & Economics : Organizational Behavior 3. Business & Economics : Management - General
ISBN: 978-1-935953-10-4

Cover design by Vanessa Perez

Printed in the United States of America

Authority Publishing
11230 Gold Express Dr. #310-413
Gold River, CA 95670
800-877-1097

Dedicated to my mom and dad, who have been an inspiration to me throughout my life. Thank you for the gift of setting such a wonderful example.

CONTENTS

ACKNOWLEDGEMENTS

There are many notable people who have been a part of my journey over the years. Each one has led to the writing of this leadership book. While I cannot recount every person, I do want to acknowledge that learning and growing comes from many different situations — some are positive, some are a struggle — but in the end they are all formative in our evolution. I would like to thank all of those people along my path — you have a part in the making of this book.

To all of those who graciously contributed through interviews and questions to help bring my thoughts and experiences to life: Fred Arcuri, Dr. Amerish Bera, Roger Box, Tara Bunch, Nora Denzel, Robert Farrell, Sandra Goldstine, Sushma Nagaraj, Jyoti Narula, Martin Nivinski, Nicole Nivinski, Dr. Claire Pomeroy, Larry Welch, Michael Ziegler.

To JT Long, my publishing consultant: without your guidance, expertise and perseverance to meet our schedule and guidelines this book would most likely still be in the making. You have been the epitome of professionalism and excellence in traveling this journey with me. I am so grateful that I had you as my partner to make my thoughts, ideas and passions come to life in this book.

To all my early readers — Dejan Milojicic, Avinash R. Mugali, Paul A. Ridge, Joe Robertson and Barbara Wakefield: thank you for your invaluable feedback with the finishing touches.

And lastly, special thanks to my husband, Craig Robertson, who has given solid support for this project and all the time I spent sequestered in my office! You are a joy in my life, each and every day.

FOREWORD

Writing a book about diversity and authenticity was not part of my long-term career plan. I was busy managing my team all over the world, raising a family and trying to be a productive member of my community. Along the way, I had a lot of time to think about what makes an effective leader. I have seen and experienced many types of leadership, some strong and successful, some weak and ineffective. They all contributed to my understanding of what is required to be a true leader. Over and over again, one of the defining features of a person who wins where others fail is the ability to embrace the concepts of diversity and authenticity.

I know, two easy words to say, but they carry a great deal of weight and must be deployed with care. To reap the benefits of a diverse organization, an authentic leader must move forward with awareness, foresight and a goal-oriented approach. Diversity cannot be a good intention that goes unmanaged. Every step must be part of a unified plan.

Likewise, coming into your own authentic self is a process to be nurtured. We all know that personal growth is a lifelong evolution. It takes thoughtful contemplation at various times in our lives to understand what we are all about and how we want to show up in the world. This is a key aspect to being a strong leader — knowing yourself and honoring all of the uniqueness that you bring to your everyday actions. Only then can you embrace the uniqueness of all of those around you and own the power of leading a diverse organization.

The good news is that all this hard work can result in a competitive edge that homogenous teams could never achieve. Diversity yields far greater creative solutions to business challenges by opening the door to an array of views from a world of perspectives. In today's business climate, that creative advantage can mean the difference between the success and the failure of an organization.

That is why I decided that I had to write this book. Diversity in the workplace is no longer something it would be nice to have. It is an imperative. Those who understand the power of a diverse, authentic organization are the ones who will shape the future. We have left one century and entered into a new one, and it is time to leave behind some old ways of thinking and move forward to explore new ideas that will serve us well going into the future.

> *Those who understand the power of a diverse, authentic organization are the ones who will shape the future.*

I hope that by sharing my passion and the best practices of some of the people I admire most in the field of diversity leadership, I can inspire at least one person to pursue the authentic path. Our world is coming together as never before. The more we understand the power of diversity and operate from our authentic selves, the better off our companies and communities will be today and tomorrow. That openness to the value each person can contribute every day is the basis of Woven Leadership.

THE LOOM

"Strength lies in differences, not in similarities."
—Stephen R. Covey

CHAPTER 1

INTRODUCTION TO WOVEN LEADERSHIP

"If we are to achieve a richer culture, rich in contrasting values, we must recognize the whole gamut of human potentialities, and so weave a less arbitrary social fabric, one in which each diverse human gift will find a fitting place." —Margaret Mead

It's time to start recognizing that leadership comes in all shapes and sizes, demographics and life experiences. We must see diversity as a secret weapon to be exploited in order to build the most successful organization. And we must also acknowledge that acting based on our own authenticity is imperative to weaving together the strength of the very fabric of the organization. We will explore why diversity and authenticity are now requirements for any organization that wants to succeed.

What does diversity leadership mean to you? Attending an annual seminar to fill a Human Resources requirement? Adding a token minority to the management team? Posting a demographically diverse picture on your web site? After almost three decades of working and leading global operations at Hewlett-Packard, I am here to tell you what "Diversity Leadership" means to me and why it should be important to you and the success of your organization.

3

The Real Definition

Diversity leadership is the art and science of bringing people with different ways of looking at the world together to weave creative solutions. Those alternative points of view can come from growing up in different cultures, generations or business units.

> *Diversity leadership is the art and science of bringing people with different ways of looking at the world together to weave creative solutions.*

You see, divergent perspectives come from more than differences in race, gender, sexual orientation or age. Everyone looks at the world through the lens of his or her own personal experience. All of those perspectives can contribute to developing and implementing innovative ways of solving problems and doing business. That is why it is essential to have lots of different points of view around the table.

The most important challenge for today's leader is to stress the positives of colorful, inclusive teams while smoothing out the wrinkles that can pop up when team members clash in approach and style. Like a modern-day Rumpelstiltskin, today's leader has to be able to take the raw materials of varied skilled employees and spin them into the gold of an efficient organization.

A Strong Framework

This process of diversity leadership goes by many names, but I call it Woven Leadership because it emphasizes the big-picture company goals while capitalizing on the unique contributions each team member makes every day.

No magic spell exists for turning straw into gold. Similarly, effective diversity leadership is not a simple sleight of hand. It is about taking the time to put in place a solid framework that brings together a well-rounded team based on trust. Individuals are accountable for reaching individual goals and everyone works for the good of the organization. Once those supports are in place, a good leader can weave in a culture based on creativity, adaptability and authentic expression. That is how effective leaders change the game to be successful in dynamic industries.

In the next seven chapters, I will share the stories from my experience as a leader and anecdotes from other leaders as the basis for stringing together strong teams. I am passionate about sharing my message that diversity is critical to any organization and its mission.

Step by Step

First, you have to start with the raw materials of skilled, educated employees from a variety of backgrounds. I made it a priority to recruit team members who were experts in their fields, as well as people with complementary skills. If I was managing a technical area, in addition to engaging technology experts, I would have other specialties such as customer service and operations people in the mix to get their perspective on how the proposed solution would impact that side of the business. Bringing together diverse perspectives generates a wider array of ideas and solutions that a more homogeneous group may overlook.

Ideally, I would surround myself with people who had more and different experience than I brought to the table. While it is always important to have the expertise necessary to run the organization's business, including relative outsiders with perspective relevant to your organization's mission will help to drive innovation. Fresh thinking paired with team members who bring years of hard-earned experience can result in whole new ways of designing, producing and delivering ideas. I'll illustrate how you further the goals of your organization by taking the time to focus on the diversity of the organization.

Once the people are in place, an effective leader establishes integrity as the centerpiece, the guiding principle of the group. Some of the best leaders in the world earn their team's trust and dedication by empowering them with difficult challenges and allowing them the freedom to learn from their mistakes. This confidence extends horizontally and vertically so the team is united in its goals, sure that management will support them when the going gets tough.

> *Some of the best leaders in the world earn their team's trust and dedication by empowering them with difficult challenges and allowing them the freedom to learn from their mistakes.*

Accountable goals are the great equalizer on a diverse team. Accountability is the anchor that keeps the team together. Holding everyone to the same standard takes the subjectivity out of management by implementing objectives and measures. By setting the goals and challenging the team to work together to advance the effort while holding each member accountable for his or her share of the work puts the shared goal in its proper place: first.

I will caution you, however, that goal-oriented does not mean leading coldly by the numbers. You can still develop and encourage employees based on their individual strengths by stepping in to coach and facilitate.

This is the foundation or the Warp of Woven Leadership and what I will cover in Part I of this book: recruiting an appropriate team for the job, fostering trust based on integrity and setting accountable goals. Once these pieces are in place, you can weave in the threads that will make the team successful.

Part II will examine the unique characteristics or the Weft: building in creativity, adaptability and authenticity that will result in a high-performing organization. Everyone wants a creative organization that can manifest solutions to reach their objectives, but unless you have put the structure in place to hold new ideas together, you will only have chaos. As you will see, creativity is not always an easy process to manage, but it is well worth the effort because it is an effective way for business to move forward. Not only is it imperative for new ideas leading to innovative solutions, it makes the process more fun.

As a leader, you have to be willing to listen to a wide array of ideas that may seem off base at first. Good ideas can come from anyone — inside or outside the team — and the trick is learning to hear the concept separate from the messenger. The result could be the key to surviving when other teams and organizations fail.

Building an organization that can adapt to the moving challenges we face in the hyper-competitive business world is critical. The individuals in the organization need to continually develop their skills and the organization needs to be positioned to develop and grow to be ready for changing situations. In order to continue reaping the benefits of your group of contrarians, you have to be willing to mix it up from time to time. I am a big proponent of investing in your people to help them grow and be ready for new opportunities. Encourage them to continue their education, attend seminars, and get recognized for their expertise inside and outside the company.

Once you have a group working like a well-oiled machine, consider mixing it up. Rotate leadership positions and bring in people who have worked with other managers to share new perspectives and ways of approaching problems. Or, consider taking on a new challenge yourself to diversify your experience and stay fresh. A good leader needs to learn to embrace change. If you lead by example, you will build credibility in the process.

The common thread running through all of these strategies is authenticity. You have to be willing to be yourself and allow your employees to bring their authentic selves to the table every day. Knowing yourself and what keeps you motivated allows you to embrace your uniqueness. Embrace the differences because those are your strategic advantages. Keeping it real allows you to connect with the people around you at a deeper level, be more effective and cut through the false fronts to solve real problems quickly. I will share stories from progressive leaders to show how being open allowed them to be more effective.

> *You have to be willing to be yourself and allow your employees to bring their authentic selves to the table every day.*

Authenticity also requires you — and your team — to do the right thing every time, even if it isn't the easiest thing. In the long run, being true to yourself is the best — and most profitable — way to lead.

The Business Case

Why is an all-inclusive approach to building teams important? Why am I so passionate about bringing fresh voices to the table? Why am I dedicated to talking to groups large and small on this subject? If you have been successful in the past, why not simply hire four more people like yourself and do more of what you have been doing? Because instead of multiplying your advantages, cloning yourself may actually handicap your efforts. Groupthink kills productivity. It has been scientifically proven.

The business world is becoming more diverse. A team that reflects the attitude and wishes of your target audience is more likely to come up with ideas for products, services, marketing and communications that appeal to them. Your customers are probably not all the same age, race and gender. By including women, minorities, and 20-, 30- and 40-somethings along with those who have traditionally made up management teams of the past, you will have a better chance of understanding and meeting the needs of the people your organization serves.

As we all know, competition is getting more intense every day. Our world is moving faster as technology evolves. Organizations must innovate beyond their current thinking of what has worked for them in the past. Only creative tension can birth the innovative ideas that will enable companies to stay on top. Diversity is not a box to be checked, but an integral step to building a strong organization that gets results. It is not only the right thing to do — it is an essential survival tactic.

Real World Experience

Why should you believe my perspective that diversity leadership is important? I worked my way up the corporate ladder over a period of 29 years. I was 19 years old when I embarked on a temp job in a suburban office of a company I had never heard of before called Hewlett-Packard. I spent three days writing part numbers on 4-inch-square cards — a job that today, ironically, would be done by the computers that my former team supported. My enthusiasm caught my supervisor's eye and he suggested I apply for a college internship the next summer. His colleague hired me that summer to do inventory. It was hot and dusty work, but I enjoyed learning and meeting the people who worked at this fast-growing company. One of the people I met was the finance controller. He hosted a brown bag lunch to talk to interns about his role at the company. I asked a lot of questions and he countered by offering me an internship the next summer as a cost accountant. I learned that I didn't want to be an accountant, but I excelled at using programs to automate the accounting processes. That attracted the attention of the IT manager, and he brought me on the following summer as a business computer programmer.

This early experience taught me that you are interviewing every day by the actions and results you achieve in your job. I also learned how important it was to enjoy what I was doing. My supervisors appreciated my enthusiasm. They were so eager to hire me that they allowed me to delay my start date by two months after graduation while I toured Europe.

I began my full-time career as a programmer analyst. I was able to build a good rapport with the internal business partners and translate their needs into automated programs. I did this by working hard to learn the systems inside and out. In the end, I earned the respect of my peers and I learned a lot about computers and people.

After four years, I decided it was time to learn something new. I became a system manager for the computers in the data center and then I moved into the telecommunications team as an engineer of the voice and data networks. I found that I had to prove myself all over again in the traditional male-oriented organization. When the opportunity to take on an additional role as customer satisfaction manager for internal IT arose, I had to overcome my boss' belief that, as a new mother, I wouldn't be interested in taking on extra responsibility. I persevered through the interview process and successfully became the program manager in charge of learning how to better serve our internal IT customers. I eventually ended up managing one of the company's first internal IT helpdesks.

I grew my leadership skills along the way by leading cross-functional, regional and global teams. I led the Americas regional organization focused on internal IT support. That was the beginning of my journey working collaboratively, not just across the company, but across cultures. It was a time of tremendous growth in my career because we had a clear definition of our destination, complete sponsorship from the executive levels of the company and everyone was on board with making it happen. This was a vivid lesson in the power of aligned goals, strong teamwork/collaboration and a commitment to attain the results.

As my career progressed and my leadership responsibilities grew, I was always eager to learn. Whether it was new technology, management skills or simply how to command attention in a room, I wanted to know more so I could be more effective.

During this time, I went through a divorce. As a single parent, I learned a lot of difficult lessons about the challenges of balancing career and home life. This was a very formidable time in my career and life, and I was fortunate to have a manager who did not see being a single mother as a limitation.

After gaining management and leadership skills, I was promoted to site IT manager and eventually the Americas User Support Center manager. In taking this opportunity, I accepted projects that seemed impossible. My diverse team not only delivered on a regional strategy to consolidate 24 helpdesks into two, we did it a week ahead of schedule with improved quality and improved internal IT customer satisfaction. That accomplishment led me to a promotion to lead the Americas region internal IT End User Support including call center and deskside support, email and file sharing and all setup services.

After the HP-COMPAQ merger I was asked to lead the Americas Front End Systems, which were the sales and marketing applications. This was a new opportunity that was not necessarily where I had set my intention but it was a good way to utilize my IT management skills and learn a new area of business. After a short time in that role I was recruited to lead the newly formed Americas Outsourcing Services to lead the Service Desk (Enterprise Helpdesk) operation. My first challenging assignment was to consolidate the operation. Employees from each company brought their own corporate culture, skills and styles. I was able to bring the team together and get them focused on shared goals, a strategy I will describe later in the book. Many of the members of my leadership team went on to new, exciting opportunities and a few grew and developed to become executives. I cherish the opportunities I had to coach this diverse group of leaders.

I was next asked to lead the Global Service Desk, which allowed me to travel all over the world. I worked with teams from India to Brazil, transforming outsource services for our customers into efficient service-oriented delivery machines.

I worked under a number of different managers with different leadership styles and philosophies. Some were very encouraging, some extremely hands-off, others had embraced a micro-managing leadership style. They all had different views on diversity. It was clear to me that growth comes not only from your job, but also learning from those you work for.

I was fortunate to be offered many different development opportunities to grow my leadership skills, including a Wharton Executive Development program that focused my career goals. All of these experiences imprinted on me new views on diversity leadership and being my authentic self as I learned to take charge of my own career and welcome opportunities that were interesting and challenging.

Regardless of where I was at in the company, I always took the time to get to know my employees, my manager and my peers on all levels. I reached out vertically and horizontally to determine where I could add value and learn from others. I developed a reputation as being collaborative and strong at building partnerships with customers and across the organization. I became "politically savvy," but at the same time always kept my forthright nature and integrity in everything I did. When I was a global manager I worked on developing the skills to be a strong candidate at the vice president level of the company.

Once I achieved my goal of becoming a vice president, I was in charge of 10,000 HP employees plus more than 4,000 contractors in more than 100 locations around the world. I was leading one of the largest call centers in the world. I carried out a very difficult set of objectives. Between 2006 and 2008 I had to make difficult choices and manage enormous change. I traveled extensively and worked over multiple time zones. I was charged with decreasing the operating budget by more than $100 million by transforming the operation all over the world.

At this point, I had a truly diverse team of managers representing many locations around the globe. In order to build camaraderie in a team with widely divergent cultures, I brought them together in one place whenever possible, incorporated formal and informal team building activities, and established the same leadership practices I will be sharing in the following pages.

I have a passion for diversity and how it is a powerful competitive advantage. In the coming decades it will take a new style of leadership to lead into the future. Through the chapters in this book I will focus on Diversity, Trust and Integrity, Accountability, Creativity, Adaptability, and Authenticity. These strands create the basis of an intricate fabric with the strength to take us to new heights and help us conquer the challenges of the future together.

Follow the Thread

In the art of weaving, the warp refers to the vertical threads on a loom that give a woven fabric its shape, and the weft is the filling or interlaced threads that run from side to side, building the design.

Section I: The Warp

"Do you wish to rise? Begin by descending. You plan a tower that will pierce the clouds? Lay first the foundation of humility." —St. Augustine

CHAPTER 2

BUILDING IN DIVERSITY

"We all should know that diversity makes for a rich tapestry, and we must understand that all the threads of the tapestry are equal in value no matter what their color." —Maya Angelou

What is diversity in an organization? The best way to define it is to explain what it isn't. Diversity isn't just a box that needs to be checked on a Human Resources form. It isn't finding that single African-American or woman to sit on the board. It isn't a picture on a web site, a lunchtime seminar or a poster in the break room. These are all visible aspects of an intentional push to include a variety of voices, but they are not diversity in and of themselves.

The mere appearance of diversity doesn't bring the real benefits of focused problem-solving possible in a heterogeneous group empowered to share their unique points of view. Only by purposefully including ideas from across the spectrum can we realize innovative solutions that will move our organization ahead of the competition.

Building diversity is everyone's responsibility. The leader, whether a program manager, first line or middle manager, or executive, has to be brave enough to share all of his or her skills and welcome a wide range of input from other team members. Managers have to be willing to put in the time to recruit and nurture diverse employees. The biggest roadblock to the flow of qualified

diverse leadership candidates is a lack of hiring and training at
the entry level. Managers at all levels can be instrumental in
driving transformation with every
hiring decision. Finally, executives

Managers have to be
willing to put in the time
to recruit and nurture
diverse employees.

have to set an example and create
a culture that welcomes all types
of employees for their ability to
deliver bottom line results.

Sandra Day O'Connor, the
first female member of the U.S. Supreme Court, said, "We don't
accomplish anything in this world alone ... and whatever happens
is the result of the whole tapestry of one's life and all the weavings
of individual threads form one to another that creates something."
From her appointment by President Ronald Reagan in 1981 to
her retirement in 2006, she worked with an increasingly diverse
court to act as the deciding vote on some of the highest profile
cases the court faced, including Boy Scouts of America v. Dale
that prohibited discrimination against troop leaders on the basis
of sexual orientation, and Bush v. Gore, which put a halt to the
Florida recount.

So what is diversity in the context of today's world — whether
it is a nonprofit, a corporation, government, or any organization
striving to make progress? Diversity requires reaching out
to people of different races, genders, cultures, experience,
personality, ages, sexual orientation and any other difference that
is unique to an individual. But it is deeper than that.

A friend and mentor, Nora Denzel, who has served in senior
executive roles at a number of technology companies, including
Intuit, compares diversity to an iceberg.

Physical appearance is just the tip of the iceberg, she points
out. The aspects of a person that lead to individual ways of looking
at problems and contributing to solutions are often hidden below

the surface. Skin color, behavior, language, actions and gender are obvious. Physical abilities, life experiences, religion, culture, values, thoughts, perspectives and sexual orientation can be below the surface. True diversity leadership means bridging the divide between the seen and unseen nature of each individual in an organization. It means valuing all of the uniqueness they have to offer.

> *True diversity leadership means bridging the divide between the seen and unseen nature of each individual in an organization. It means valuing all of the uniqueness they have to offer.*

People draw on their backgrounds as templates for assessing, predicting and acting in future situations. Because people from different cultures often experience different challenges in life, they can bring the unique lessons they learned to the table and predict problems that others would never have imagined because they had not "walked a mile in those shoes."

There is no one right mix of these elements for a productive team member. Only the interplay with other members where all are encouraged to draw on the reservoir of their backgrounds will result in an initiative that can cut through the clutter and turn the organization in the right direction.

A Competitive Imperative

Why is diversity a competitive imperative? The word "diversity" has become political as legislation requiring quotas can polarize people. This rule-based approach is a world apart from the reality of creating a culture where diverse people feel valued.

Successful organizations don't create diverse teams for the sake of diversity. Leveraging the power of differences and similarities to achieve a common goal — Nora calls this "Inclusion" — is a powerful force. Studies show the more diverse the team, the better the results.

Going back to 1995, a study by Peter Wright, Steven Ferris, Janine Hiller and Mark Kroll called "Competitiveness Through Management of Diversity: Effects of Stock Price Valuation" showed that stock prices were higher for companies that had what the U.S. Department of Labor called "exemplary affirmative action programs." That result was echoed in a similar study called "Wall Street Likes Its Women: An Examination of Women in the Top Management Teams of Initial Public Offerings" by Theresa Welbourne in 2000. Welbourne reported that having a diverse management team at the time of the initial public offering of a company's stock results in a higher stock price than that received by similar companies with more homogeneous management teams.

A year later, a study called "Workforce Diversity and Productivity: An Analysis of Employer-Employee Matched Data" by Kenneth Troske showed that both manufacturing and service companies showed positive and significant increased productivity when they had more diverse workforces.

The trick to attracting more women, minorities and other diverse groups to the executive suite is to create a workplace that is nurturing for all and then develop that talent across the board. A 2010 study by The Executive Search Group showed that while 80 percent of HR leaders said a gender-diverse talent pool is an advantage, many complained they had difficulty finding and retaining qualified candidates for C Level positions. The study pointed to lack of recognition and/or flexibility as one of the reasons women leave companies before making it to the leadership level. Instituting family-friendly practices can keep more men and women on the management track, thus expanding the pool of potential future leaders.

The Power of Different

Working with a diverse team is not only the right thing to do socially, it is the right thing to do for the bottom line. Why is that? Think about your customer base. In today's global world, if your workforce doesn't represent your audience and partners, then how are you going to be able to understand them — and meet their needs?

Having someone on your team who intuitively understands the culture could save you millions of dollars — and your reputation. I can't help but think that if General Motors had more Latinas in their development department, they would have renamed the Nova before shipping it south of the border with a brand that translated to "no-go." Before manufacturing a shipload of merchandise and loading it onto a cargo ship, wouldn't it be nice to know if the smiles and nods from that Japanese buyer really meant yes?

Around the globe, laws, customs and religious beliefs can create barriers that require a level of sensitivity to operate legally and safely while staying true to your values. In some countries, a person can go to jail for being gay or lesbian. Encouraging employees to be open about their lifestyle in the workplace there could literally be putting their lives in danger. You have to be accommodating of their needs while also protecting their interests.

And diversity in some cultures is much more nuanced than in others. Two people who may look the same to an American may come from two different castes, tribes or families and bring a tradition of tension that has to be dealt with constructively in order to create a productive workplace.

While globalization brings challenges to developing diversity, it also brings enormous benefits. In fact diversity is a competitive imperative. The equation is more complex, but the rewards are greater.

Fresh Perspective

Statistics show that we have a long way to go before our executive offices reflect the marketplace in a meaningful way. In the U.S. alone, female buyers influence 95 percent of all purchases and control 80 percent of household spending, but a University of California, Davis study in 2009 concluded that only slightly more than 10 percent of the top 400 companies in California have females in board seats or top executive roles. Nearly a third had no women board directors and no women executive officers. In fact, the number of women on boards had dropped slightly from the previous year. How can you market to such a powerful audience if your team doesn't reflect people who intimately understand these buyers' needs, wants and desires?

The same goes for young people. The 37 million 25- to 35-year-olds who control $1.1 trillion in annual income view advertising, technology and consumerism in a different way than the generations that went before them does. If you are going to successfully sell to this market, you need to include representatives of this contingent in your employee roster and engage them at various levels.

The generation entering the workforce now is wildly different than those who entered the workforce 30 years ago. Organizations need to embrace this demographic and its unique approach to business. We need to listen to what they have to say, include them in our leadership teams and develop their leadership potential. They may not yet have the experience of a long-term career, but they do have their own unique perspectives and they interact with technology in ways we have not seen in the past. In order to understand more about the perspective of young people in the organization I asked Sushma Nagaraj, a young leader at HP in India, how the workplace will change with young leaders in the organization. She described young leaders as energetic and ready to take on new challenges. They connect both on a professional and a personal level by taking the time to share their interests to build the rapport needed to create a strong performing team. Young leaders understand how to connect to the incoming workforce. My daughter, Nicole Nivinski, recently promoted to supervisor at her company, explained the importance of including multigenerational perspectives in the workplace this way: "It's important to get fresh ideas from young people. They look at things in a different way and work with technologies in a much broader way than generations before. Don't discard their input; it may be a new perspective that has never been considered that could lead to great possibilities."

Maintaining a steady flow of young people coming into an organization helps achieve diversity of thought and keeps the energy and enthusiasm of the team at a high level.

Looking back to when I was entering the workplace after college, I recall a similar sense of excitement about life both in the office and outside the workplace. Maintaining a steady flow of young people coming into an organization helps achieve diversity of thought and keeps the energy and enthusiasm of the team at a high level. This brings new ideas to the table and creates an atmosphere in which creativity thrives.

Young people are redefining how we do business. This young generation is highly tech savvy, desires work-life balance and extreme multitasking. We need to be inclusive of this unique population in our workforce to realize their competitive advantage.

Troske's study of workplace diversity showed that the percent of recent college graduates in a company positively impacted productivity. Organizations cannot afford to ignore this progressive insight. A mix of generations working side by side helps bring ideas and perspectives from all angles, allowing you to arrive at a stronger solution.

Beyond Visible

As I said before, however, diversity goes beyond the visible. To use a sports analogy, you wouldn't want a football team made up exclusively of quarterbacks, even if they were all great quarterbacks. You need someone to protect your passer, someone to catch the ball and someone to kick the conversion point. These are all specific skills and take very different approaches that work together to reach the ultimate goal.

The number of personality tests out there seems to multiply every year and the names or colors used to try to put people into manageable boxes are as varied as the number of people in a given company. People are complex, living, changing beings who are not easily labeled. However, when assembling your team, I have found that reaching out to a mix of people who might be considered introverted, extroverted, analytical and creative, for instance, can give you access to the widest array of approaches to a job. That is a lot more productive than surrounding yourself with people just like you — and much more interesting. You will be in an organization where you can learn from them every day. That is the power of a diverse team.

At one point in my career a senior executive said: "Hire people who are not like yourself." I took this advice and truly embraced the concept. We have a natural tendency to hire people who make you feel comfortable because they have similar styles, interests or other attributes. But hiring these "ditto" people may not be what's best for the overall mix of the organization. It is not to say that they would not add value. But would they add the most value? Or would someone with a different style and strengths bring a new mix to the team? Ever since that talk, I have become conscious of asking this question whenever I make a personnel decision. At times I hired or promoted someone who was extremely sharp but had a difficult personality. This person would bring new ideas and challenge the status quo. Certainly, the hire would bring along some management challenges as well. However, I was committed to coaching the person to be as effective as possible. The investment was always worth it.

The Gift of Understanding

My parents gave me a gift as I was growing up, the gift of being colorblind. At a time when racial segregation was threatening to tear apart our country, our home was without slander and hate. We were raised to not judge people by their outward appearance, but to get to know them and understand the similarities we might have.

In 1969, when I was 9 years old, we moved to Alabama for a year. Segregation had recently been determined by a court to be illegal, but at school, the old divisions were still very prevalent. My sisters and I were perplexed. Why were there two drinking fountains? Two bathrooms? And, at the end of the day, why did the black kids get on one bus and the white kids on another? The tension had made its way from the homes to the schoolyard. When we came home on the first day of school, I asked my mom the reasons behind the segregation I had seen. My mother did the best she could, but there is no easy way to explain to a 9-year-old why people have hate based on a phantom set of fears.

This experience at a young age made a profound impact on me. I am so grateful that my parents insulated us and taught us to be open. Although I could not name the attribute as a child, being "colorblind" has been a priceless gift. It has enabled me to keep an open mind and helped me look beyond the surface of so many situations to see the true beauty that lies within. And it has given me the chance to experience people and cultures around the world with a child-like wonder.

I have embraced this gift throughout my life and career. During the time I was responsible for more than 10,000 HP employees and more than 4,000 contracted employees in more than 100 locations around the world, I traveled extensively. I seized every opportunity to learn about the various cultures and people in order to better understand how to motivate my organization and drive business objectives more effectively. For instance, while leading the call center operations, I learned how many holidays around the world are faith-based. If we employed people with different religious backgrounds, we could more effectively cover the holidays and preserve the employee wishes to take off work to be with their families. In our call center in India we had a mixture of various faiths. When a faith-based holiday was coming up, we made sure that employees from other faiths would be there to cover. This is a simple example of the power of diverse teams.

Managing diversity is a strategic weapon. When used effectively it can be a powerful force in reaching your objectives.

Managing diversity is a strategic weapon. When used effectively it can be a powerful force in reaching your objectives.

Filters

We all have filters we use to view the world. These filters originate from every aspect of our lives: experiences we've had, people we've known, things we were raised to believe, ingrained cultural norms. It is human nature to operate based on preconceived notions about particular situations. Only a conscious effort can break through these filters and see things for their real business implications.

When I traveled around the world as a global operations manager, I was acutely aware of the diverse cultural customs in each country. For example, I was traveling to Tunisia to do an operations review during the time of Ramadan. Ramadan is a Muslim holiday that lasts for about a month. Fasting is a part of the custom; no food or drink can be consumed from sun-up until sundown. Luckily, I was well briefed on this prior to arriving and carefully refrained from eating and drinking with the team during the day in order to be respectful.

By paying attention to cultural nuances, I was able to engage without offending those in my organization or customer base. I took the time to understand what steps needed to be taken to bring people together. This allowed me to build a strong, inclusive team and build rapport with all the folks across the global operation. The result was an organization that is open to all perspectives and opinions and does so from a place of respect for the differences as well as the similarities that they all share.

Finish Work

While at HP, I often stepped in to lead an organization that had been created before my arrival. More often than not, the teams would be dominated by men and lacking other types of diversity, as well. This was common in the technology field. I would painstakingly remix the team with diversity as one of my goals. I would recruit team members from different backgrounds, cultures, gender, personality styles and work experiences. My goal was to infuse the organization with the creative thinking that a diverse array of thinkers brings to the table. It was not always easy. When the team was coming together, we would need to take time for the team members to understand each other. The result would be a team that was more powerful for its differences and ready to produce in new and unique ways.

If a team is truly diverse, there will be challenges initially because everyone interacts in different ways. But, in the end, each member will be stronger for the experience. Diverse teams need more opportunities to work together. The process of spending time together allows the team to see the value each person brings. Team-building activities that allow members to see other sides of their coworkers can speed up the melding process.

Diversity initiatives lose their power, however, if they aren't applied fairly. A colleague and friend, Tara Bunch, vice president of consumer support operations at Hewlett-Packard, shared her insight on treating everyone equally. As an openly lesbian woman, she was naturally sensitive to the needs of the LBGT (lesbian, bisexual, gay and transgender) community. However, at one point, she found herself in a difficult situation. She was managing a team where a significant portion was part of a conservative Christian men's group focused on empowering men to be the head of the household. After some complaints, management banned the members of the organization from wearing t-shirts and using coffee mugs with the group logo because some other members of the team felt uncomfortable with the message of male dominance. Bunch considered the situation from all perspectives and decided that as long as the men were respectful, everyone — whether members of conservative Christian or Pride groups — should be allowed to express themselves. She talked it over with management and they agreed. "That created a level of tolerance that made everyone feel welcome," she shared.

As you can see, diversity leadership is not always easy. The rules of who to hire, the divergent voices at meetings and a constant struggle to balance individual needs can be intense. But the results can be spectacular.

Like weaving a tapestry, you first have to start with a plan for what the piece will look like when it is finished. Then pick the raw materials based on your desired outcome. Think about the various aspects of experience, culture and other attributes that will saturate your organization with the richness of a wide array of resources. That is how you weave your team into a stronger finished piece.

CHAPTER 3

TRUST AND INTEGRITY AT THE CENTER

"Sometimes you can't see yourself clearly until you see yourself through the eyes of others." —*Ellen DeGeneres*

O nce you have your diverse organization in place, how do you get everyone united to reach the organization's goals? The next structural element that needs to be put in place is trust and integrity. Trust is the uncompromising belief that you will always act with integrity, and conversely, that your organization will do the same. This two-way street of trust is earned over time through each interaction. It is hard won and easily lost, but a key aspect of an effective leader.

Word of Honor

Trust starts with being honest with your employees. I led the shift to outsourced and offshored operations during a challenging time in the IT Industry. My job was often to deliver news about strategy changes with our operational structure that led to job loss. I could have hinted at possible decisions and sugarcoated the truth for as long as possible, but that would have made matters worse for my organization. And I probably wouldn't have been fooling anyone. Most people can sense when you are lying or telling half-truths. This scent of dishonesty can spur rumors worse than the truth and destroy your credibility before you even get started. It can also lead to passive — and sometimes not so passive — resistance and undermine an already difficult transition. Keeping open communication whenever possible will alleviate confusion and doubt amongst the troops. I grew up with a strong example of trust and integrity. My father was an admiral in the United States Navy. He had a distinguished career with a long list of impressive accomplishments. Although I was always proud of these accolades, I learned as I went along in my own journey that one of the most important examples my father gave me was in the area of trust and integrity. I often sought counsel from my father during challenging times in my career. His experience of leading military operations on a large scale during crisis situations was filled with real-life lessons. One was the fact that the people you lead can see through you when you are not being up-front and honest with them. He knew that he could lose his team's support if he didn't act with trust and integrity.

People you lead can see through you when you are not being up-front and honest with them.

I led many transformation initiatives during my career and I knew that building trust with the team was imperative. The best way to do that was to be open about what was happening every step of the way. I shared as much of the logic behind the decisions as possible so people could understand the business imperative. It was important for them to understand the options and why the strategies were important to remain competitive. I found that even when the outcomes for individual employees were not desirable, if they knew the business case and the thoughts that led to the decision, they could at least accept it from a business perspective.

Without this understanding, it can often feel personal or ill-conceived. This honesty allowed employees to make decisions about their futures based on the best information available with as much lead time as possible. It wasn't easy, but it was a basis to build trust with my team. A colleague, Tara Bunch, called it "treating employees as partners for change rather than recipients of change." Bunch practiced this through major innovation of the Consumer Support organization at HP. She engaged all levels of her organization and her key partners as well. In doing this, she was very successful in executing her plans.

The same is true on an individual level. There were times when I would have a leader on my staff who was excellent in many ways, but lacking in a few key areas. One leader in particular got results, met deadlines, went above and beyond by working long hours, but in the process compromised relationships with peers to get the job done. These peers became frustrated and did not want to work with this person again on future projects. Clearly this individual would have been much more effective if she had built a positive rapport with her coworkers. I very candidly coached her about how she was perceived by her peers. I suggested how she could be more effective if she collaborated constructively across the organization. I gave specific examples of her interactions and why they were disruptive. I asked her to go and talk to the very people she was having conflict with and openly discuss the dissension and how they could work better together. Like many of the people I coached, she was surprised by the feedback. She tried to debate and minimize her behavior, but I continued to give examples that illustrated where she needed to improve and stressed the benefit she would see by changing her approach.

Most people want to excel in what they do, and even if personal interaction is uncomfortable, they need to address their approach and improve if they want to be successful in the position. It is very rewarding to coach someone to reach beyond his or her current possibilities. It is even more rewarding when colleagues who had previously given feedback on the person you are coaching say they have seen a change for the better.

Everyone has a very high potential to succeed. Sometimes, all it takes is a mentor or manager willing to take the time and have the harsh discussion that allows that person to step into his or her leadership potential.

If an employee is simply a bad fit and not meeting the standards of the team, honesty is still the most respectful approach. The employee can leave, voluntarily or involuntarily, or he or she can take a close look at where improvement and changes can be made.

Many people are uncomfortable giving constructive feedback. Over the course of my career, I've managed many people. Often, my feedback was as a surprise to the person receiving it, even though a candid conversation with previous managers mirrored the same problem areas. It isn't fair to your employee to withhold feedback, no matter how difficult it is to give. How can people improve if they are not given an honest reflection of how they are perceived? When an organization is open to individual and team feedback, it accelerates the growth of the organization as a whole. Feedback is seen as a way to help build overall performance.

Receiver

A leader also has to be able to hear the truth. Tara Bunch, the manager mentioned above, preached the power of honest brainstorming. She would create an environment where lively debate was celebrated. Employees were encouraged to bring ideas that conflicted with her own. The pros and cons were sorted out, considered and improved upon by the group. Then they would decide together and move forward.

A leader's reaction to that first person who challenges the manager can set the stage for the life of the group. If a question is shot down without being given due consideration, then others will be hesitant to ask questions. Why should they? This can lead to stagnation. If the suggestion is embraced or discarded based on its merits rather than who made the suggestion, then a climate of

> *If the leader had all the answers, he or she wouldn't need an organization.*

acceptance is created that can lead to results far beyond what any one member — including the leader — could achieve alone.

Many times there is an incorrect assumption that the leader is searching for a certain answer. I would impress upon my team that I can always come up with a plan or solution, but it may not be the best. You take the time to carefully craft a dynamic, diverse team of top-notch performers because you want their collective experience and wisdom. If the leader had all the answers, he or she wouldn't need an organization. Each member's candid ideas are critical to the outcome.

This cooperative approach only works, however, if that final step is enforced. While debate may be encouraged during the meeting, a good leader helps everyone agree on a decision and pledge to move forward together in full support. Sometimes not everyone can agree and a decision needs to be made. It is important for the organization to commit to the decision completely once the decision is made. While this isn't always easy for those who dissent, it is critical to move the organization forward.

Arm's Length

Sometimes, the best way to show your trust in an employee is to let him or her fail.

Booker T. Washington, the famous civil rights leader, understood the importance of earning and giving trust. He was the son of a slave woman and a white man and was 8 years old when slaves were legally emancipated. He collaboratively worked with some of the wealthiest white Northerners and the founders of the African-American movement to fund schools for African-Americans looking for their place in a new, free, but segregated world. How did he inspire confidence in a nation torn about the right thing to do? He inspired trust through his words and his actions. He worked to unite a torn country by bringing people together with a common cause.

Sometimes that meant respecting the different approaches of fellow civil rights leaders to achieve the common goal of eventual equality. He took a lot of criticism at times for his approach, but he never wavered in his dedication.

Washington's ability to help people coalesce around an idea was described in this famous quote: "Few things help an individual more than to place responsibility upon him, and to let him know that you trust him."

That ability to challenge individuals and support their work, regardless of the outcome, is as true for a social leader as a business leader. Employees tasked with pioneering new methods have to be given the freedom to make — and learn from — mistakes with the full backing of their superiors. As my son, Martin Nivinski, once put it, "We don't learn from our mistakes by simply making them; but understanding them is where the lesson exists."

At times it is the very act of making a "mistake" that leads us to the innovation we are striving to achieve. Part of building trust is to support team members while they are "learning from their mistakes." This will encourage them to continue to strive hard and also teach them to course-correct when plans lead to an undesirable outcome.

Obviously you need to protect the organization's interest from impending disaster; I am not implying that you throw all caution to the wind. But there needs to be some leeway to allow your team to take risks. I always appreciated working in an environment where I could take calculated risks. There would be certain expectations that had to be met, but there were also areas in which we could be innovative. At times, we would have to quickly course-correct if a plan proved to be inadequate. However, it is important to have the ability to test-market, prototype or pilot an idea for proof of concept.

By setting up clear boundaries of what is acceptable and what is required, and then giving employees the freedom to find their own way within those boundaries, you empower them to come up with solutions and be creative.

By setting up clear boundaries of what is acceptable and what is required, and then giving employees the freedom to find their own way within those boundaries, you empower them to come up with solutions and be creative. Particularly, when you are leading an organization where the people are dispersed over a wide geographic area, micromanaging doesn't work. Only by focusing on goals and giving guidelines and the tools to make it happen can everyone in the organization be successful.

Team members must understand your expectations and how you will hold them accountable. They also have to be able to count on your word that you will be there to support them no matter what the outcome. This is how a leader builds a strong team that can move fast and be successful.

Where Credit Is Due

Business guru Peter F. Drucker said, "The leaders who work most effectively, it seems to me, never say 'I.' And that's not because they have trained themselves not to say 'I.' They don't think 'I.' They think 'we'; they think 'team.' They understand their job to be to make the team function. They accept responsibility and don't sidestep it, but 'we' gets the credit. This will create trust, what enables you to get the task done."

An effective team-oriented leader shows his employees that he is willing to do whatever he is asking his team to do. I had an excellent example of this when working under a vice president at HP, Tay Peng Ooi, who was from Singapore. Ooi set a standard for work ethic around the concept of being dedicated and working just as hard as anyone on his team. He set a high standard for the team, but it was clear that the standard for himself was as high or higher. There were many times that the goals he set for the organization were very challenging and he was always there beside anyone on the team to work to reach the collective goals. It was not uncommon for Ooi to travel to a meeting where his team was working on strategies and objectives so that he could be interactive and support in whatever way necessary. Ooi was by far one of the hardest-working people I've met. It was an honor to work for someone who was so selfless in his leadership. Ooi passed away in 2009 but left a leadership legacy of trust and respect to all who knew him.

Integrity as a Business Tool

In the end, the ability to earn the trust of your team comes from your dedication to leading with integrity. Nora Denzel may have said it best when she said, "Integrity is not just about not cheating or stealing; personal integrity is living without compromise, saying what needs to be said right away, not what people want to hear. Say the same thing in private that you would in public." What you say and do need to be the same thing.

When faced with a difficult decision, ask yourself — and your team — what is the right thing to do? If you use this as the benchmark every time, then you will be consistent and your team will have faith in you.

It is essential that "what you say and what you do" are consistent. This is vital to building trust in an organization. The people who are in the organization will see through any discrepancy and it will tear apart the effectiveness of the team. I have had examples throughout my career where people would

> *Once the leader has opened the door to a substandard way of operating, the downstream effects will permeate throughout the actions of the entire organization.*

say what they were going to do and then not follow through. Whether this is a peer, manager or employee, it sets the tone for the relationships from that point forward. There are obvious consequences in some cases.

You may have good employees who decide to go elsewhere because they could not tolerate the inconsistencies and lack of integrity. And there may be more pervasive consequences like setting the tone and behaviors for your organization. This is a dangerous place to be, a Pandora's box that cannot be closed. Once the leader has opened the door to a substandard way of operating, the downstream effects will permeate throughout the actions of the entire organization.

You do not have to look far to see examples of companies who went down this path and ended up with disastrous consequences.

Possibly the most well known case in point is Enron and the demise of the company due to their unethical financial practices. Leadership and organizational change consultant A.J. Schuler pointed to a flawed corporate culture at Enron that lacked integrity from the top down and valued growth by any means.

Shortly after the company collapsed, Schuler wrote, "Enron's corporate culture best exemplified values of risk taking, aggressive growth and entrepreneurial creativity. These are all positive values. But these values were not balanced by genuine attention to corporate integrity and the creation of customer — not just shareholder —value. Because the Enron corporate culture was not well grounded, a single scorecard — maximized price per share of common stock — became its reason for being, and even its positive values became liabilities." There is also a side benefit to acting with integrity — you can be at ease with your actions knowing that you are being true to yourself and everyone around you. When people lack integrity, they have to constantly look over their shoulder. A leader who acts with uncompromising integrity is always consistent — the team knows what to expect from their leader. The leader sets the tone for the organization. Integrity must be expressed in every action. Without integrity, the organization will be dysfunctional and the results will be sub-optimized.

At times, employees may fear the consequences of being honest. Reporting negative news to a manager can be difficult. I made a point of being approachable if "bad news" needed to be shared. I stressed to my employees that I wanted to get a "heads-up" if there was a metric that was not performing or a customer escalation looming. Even though we had monthly business and operational metric reviews, I would expect folks on my staff to let me know between reviews if there was a metric that was in a downward trend and needed attention. That way I could know what to expect and help with resources as much as possible to get it back on track. I also wanted to know if there was a customer escalation. Asking for these two pieces of information gave a two-way dialogue with my team, signaling that it was okay to bring up bad news. In fact, it was expected. This created an atmosphere of candor. I always fostered an attitude of "no surprises." It was important to me to have a finger on the pulse of the organization. Keeping the dialogue open and often made it easier for my team to bring up challenging topics.

In weaving circles, the structural integrity of the fabric is determined by how closely the threads are woven. A loose weave is considered unattractive, cheap. Only when all of the cords are aligned and tightly knit will they be able to wear well over the long-term. The same is true in organizations. A tightly woven team where each member relies on the others to do the right thing, and carry their share of the weight, is stronger than any one member alone.

CHAPTER 4

ACCOUNTABILITY IS KEY

"What gets measured gets done." —*John E. Jones*

A well-woven tapestry will not only stand the test of time and durability, but also increase in beauty and value. Similarly, a well-woven team will stand strong and even improve during challenging business cycles. An organization needs a strong structure to give form to the diverse solutions that come out of the creative teams working together day-in and day-out.

Crafting a diverse team outfitted with the latest in trust-building techniques does not ensure you will reach the intended results. While the raw materials of a great team are wonderful, they can only succeed if you give them a solid framework.

We have all seen charismatic leaders who have an uncanny ability to draw people to them, yet without clear directions and goals, structured review and accountability, they fail. Creating a structure with objectives and targets that are well understood by everyone on the team and having those objectives and targets cascade throughout the organization is the foundation of a winning framework.

While working backward from a set target might seem obvious to some, it is not always a pervasive practice. Countless organizations fail in their pursuit of progress due to a lack of goals, or too poorly thought-out goals. Loosely defined or conflicting goals are worse in the long run. Only a well-organized system of checks and balances will support the dynamic team we all want to lead.

Successfactors and Workforce Intelligence Institute studied performance management and how alignment with goals affected the outcome of success. The study revealed that 67 percent of companies with stronger financial performance cover all managers and some levels below with a performance management system. Conversely, only 28 percent of the weaker performers use some sort of formal evaluation process. In addition, the study found 44 percent of the stronger performers have almost 100 percent aligned goals at the managerial level, while none of the weaker performers took the time to make sure everyone was working toward the same result. These studies illustrate the strong cause and effect of measuring and aligning goals at all levels.

> *Countless organizations fail in their pursuit of progress due to a lack of goals, or too poorly thought-out goals. Loosely defined or conflicting goals are worse in the long run.*

Setting individual and shared goals — and then holding everyone on the team accountable — is imperative to achieving organizational success.

Focusing on agreed-upon goals that are aligned throughout the organization takes the subjectivity out of leadership and replaces the vague — and potentially biased — system of inconsistent rewards with objective measurements that each member can own. This levels the playing field and ensures everyone is treated fairly.

Measured Success

I learned about the importance of treating everyone fairly early in life as I watched my mother, Sandra Goldstine, build and lead a productive organization in the male-dominated mortgage banking industry. In the late 1960s, her rise to the position of regional vice president was an exception to the status quo. Few women achieved that kind of stature. She worked hard, knew her business and nurtured her employees.

She not only hired experienced applicants, she was also willing to train those with the potential and ambition to learn. My mother had a belief that she continually reinforced: "What gets measured gets done." This mantra has stuck with me throughout my career. It is simple, yet powerful. The premise is that if it is important that something get done, then take the time to put measures in place to manage it. Many businesses struggle with competing priorities; a measurement and review system helps to keep the main priorities in focus. It is a guiding light to the organization.

Goldstine had five account executives under her and they had another 15 loan officers under them. She sat with each executive at the beginning of the quarter to set goals together. At the end of the period they compared their success against the state of the industry and talk about what needed to change to reach the goals next time. The mortgage business is very intense and fast paced. Implementing a strong measurement system allowed her employees to work on what they needed to without interacting constantly throughout the goal period. Goldstine was there to support them, but didn't need to get involved in the details.

She was goal-oriented early in her career. That laser focus and can-do attitude kept her team motivated to find new ways to succeed. These are the same tools that work to keep a diverse team pointed in the right direction.

Purpose Driven

Later, my manager at HP, former Vice President Larry Welch, used to say that it is not a natural act for a random group of people to wholeheartedly take on a collective job unless a leader shows the members of the team why they are dependent on each other for their individual success. A leader has to convince every member of the team that they can accomplish more together than if they worked individually.

> *A leader has to convince every member of the team that they can accomplish more together than if they worked individually.*

His advice? "Start with the purpose, then measure the outcome in whatever metrics are most important to the goal." These need to be actionable goals. The success of a team depends on its ability to get things done. Business reports and reviews are an important part of holding the team and individuals accountable. They are the building blocks for a successful organization.

Welch put in place rigorous measurement systems and held his team accountable with monthly reviews. This was an inclusive process that the team would go through to commit to the goals. He also ensured that diversity of the organization was managed throughout the year. Specific metrics were created and reviewed each month. He led by example, building a diverse management team and holding others accountable for similar diversity goals. The importance of building a team with different perspectives, backgrounds, ethnicity and gender was stressed. This was not an occasional conversation at a staff meeting; it was a business imperative. Whenever there was an opportunity to hire at any level in the organization, Welch wanted to know what the impact on diversity would be. He would ask the hiring manager for a

plan and review the diversity goals. He expected that when a
management position opened on the team, his managers would
have been developing employees to be prepared for the opportunity
and ensure that all employees were considered for the best possible
diversity outcome along with the best possible person for the
position. It was a strong show of diversity leadership — he meant
what he said and he backed it up with consistent action.

Many times you hear organizations say that they are not
diverse because the candidates coming to them are not diverse. This
is often a red herring. If you are earnest about building diversity,
you look at ways to build your feeder pools of candidates. This
long-term diversity vision drove Welch's expectation. That is why
he continues to be an inspiration for "walking the talk," in other
words leading by example.

No Boundaries

The best results I have ever delivered were when I was given a
number and a date. I excel when there are no boundaries on how
to achieve a particular goal by a particular date. I led through
the boom and the bust of the '80s, '90s and the first decade of
the 21st century. The goals were either "grow," which translated
into "expand capacity rapidly" or "reduce," which translated
into "quickly determine where costs can be cut." Either way, the
imperative was the same: drastic action to change course needed
to happen quickly while also maintaining or improving customer
satisfaction. When these objectives were given, I saw them as a
challenge to overcome. At initial meetings, my team would first
express the reasons why it would be impossible to deliver. Each
of these seemingly impossible obstacles were noted, and then we
would create plans to address them one by one.

These initial sessions proved important for two reasons. First, the team needed to get over the shock of what they were being asked to do. Second, they had to vent their concerns and frustrations. This is an important part of the problem-solving process. Skipping over this evaluation step would deny an outlet for their concerns, and the opportunity to address problems proactively. It starts the process of building a plan that everyone can embrace.

One of my favorite assignments early in my executive IT career at HP came in the late '90s. I was leading the internal IT call center operation across North and South America. This involved Canada, the U.S. and several countries across Latin America. Four different languages had to be accommodated. In addition, there were many business units with different business imperatives. In my new role, I was tasked with consolidating 24 independently run internal IT helpdesks into one call center operation in two locations for redundancy. The objective was to reduce the operating expense significantly while improving the end-user support experience — a very reasonable objective. What complicated it was that in order to meet financial commitments, it had to occur within 12 weeks.

The challenges were many: telecommunications infrastructure, staffing, training and change management with the users at each site. This is where creative solutions are critical to meeting objectives. Employing practices suitable for a less aggressive goal would not deliver the results in the timeline required. We had to come up with plans that had never been tried before.

The team, which included participants from across all the sites, gathered in multiple teleconference sessions. The planning sessions were led with "no boundary" discussions. "What do you need to make this happen?" I asked over and over. Then we would look at all the various options and work through the best plan. It takes strong leadership to be open to a wide range of ideas while weighing possible risks. Sometimes an idea will have unacceptable consequences, but that can only be determined after it is examined. I was dedicated to exploring widely before narrowing in on the right set of plans. Everything was evaluated based on the idea's ability to deliver the measurable goals.

We decided to bring together the call center agents from one of the sites that would be merging and have them work at that new site before and after the transition. This gave the customers a seamless experience. It gave the new call center support agents valuable expertise beyond the classroom experience while they got up to speed with their skills. We worked with the telecom companies on what needed to occur and they brought in solutions to meet the capacity as we transitioned.

People think differently when they don't have boundaries. When people have been so focused on working a certain way over time, they tend to huddle in their box. Then work begins to be measured against the method rather than the outcome. That doesn't

> *"By making your employees more accountable, you make your organization more productive."*

work in today's fast-paced world of maximum results. Only with a wide-open discussion where everyone is encouraged to speak up for the sake of the common goal will you produce the result that enables you to leap ahead of the competition.

Big Goals

Shared accountability is not a new idea. Jack Welch, the legendary CEO of General Electric, famously said, "By making your employees more accountable, you make your organization more productive." Welch used accountability in his quest to turn GE into one of the most successful companies in the world. When he was appointed CEO of the company in 1981, it had a market capitalization of $13 billion and its fingers in dozens of industries as diverse as turbines, household appliances, media and insurance. When Welch retired in 2001, GE's capitalization was $500 billion. In 2010, Forbes ranked the company as the second largest in the world.

Welch challenged each business unit to either be one of the top two in its space or get out of that business. That simple rule allowed him to clearly communicate his commitment to being the best. It also allowed him to use his resources wisely. He could objectively determine where it was worth investing to improve, and where to cut losses. He had to make some difficult decisions, but putting a number to his vision helped everyone understand why he was taking drastic action — he would settle only for the best.

The challenge with accountability is that you have to be bold and publicly announce what you want to do, give your team the tools to do it and then deal with the consequences if they don't reach those goals.

Only by analyzing the performance of the whole system can a leader determine which pieces are working and which ones need to be replaced. This process can take time. In a large organization it can be difficult to make changes quickly, but the faster the right team is in place, the sooner the intended results will take shape.

Many times in my career I have had to make adjustments to the resources on the team because results were not being accomplished. Sometimes it was a process that failed. Other times it was an individual who didn't have the skill for the particular position. That sometimes meant taking the difficult step of removing the poor performer and bringing in a stronger fit for the job.

No one enjoys firing an employee. However, for the good of the organization, the team and the employees, sometimes parting ways is the only solution. Fred Arcuri, a senior vice president at the telecommunications company SureWest Communications, told me that he seldom had a problem letting people go because he set expectations so clearly that once the situation had been explained, people would end up quitting on their own. "I just had to do the paperwork," he said.

Arcuri created a culture of accountability by earning the respect of his employees. He worked his way up from a position as telephone lineman over 30 years. And he consistently set and enforced rules so that no one could accuse him of favoritism. When expectations are clear, leading becomes a lot easier.

Arcuri knew what all good leaders know. Goals are made to be met and leaders are there to ensure they are met.

Identifying a performance problem can be challenging because so many dynamics come into play, some emotional and subjective. Using measurable goals helps keep the conversation objective and the results positive. Make the determination based on the big picture and take action quickly. It is not fair to the rest of the team when one person consistently fails to meet commitments. You cannot compromise the performance of the organization for one person. It will cause frustration and distract the organization as a whole.

Leading With Heart

Don't misunderstand me here. Holding a team accountable for shared goals does not mean you have to coldly lead by the numbers. You can still support and encourage employees based on their development opportunities. Accountability sets the "what" of your goals. Coaching gives your team the opportunity to find their personal "how" of reaching those goals.

Larry Welch, the HP executive I mentioned previously, helped me reach my goals by giving me the tools I needed to succeed in the next level in my career. He understood that it was in the company's best long-term interest to nurture talent in addition to meeting short-term goals. He would look for people with passion, talent and a desire to learn and grow and invest in them.

At a large company, entire departments are often dedicated to recruiting and training diverse teams, but even the smallest organization can take the time to encourage employees to reach higher.

When I was a first level manager and reporting to Welch, he asked me one day, "How can I help you break through the glass ceiling?" This question caught me off-guard but made me contemplate what I saw as barriers to my advancement, and also helped me have a meaningful coaching session with him. I explained to him how at times I would express an idea and it would not get attention from the team. Then, when one of my male peers would make the same suggestion, there would be interest. Welch and I then worked on how I could be heard in these discussions. It was a pivotal discussion for both of us. It gave him the awareness to watch the dynamic of the team. He coached and developed me to have a much bolder presence and leadership style. I learned to be more confident and definitive in how I raised ideas in our discussions. Over time I became a much stronger presence on the team.

> *Coaching gives your team the opportunity to find their personal "how" of reaching those goals.*

We also discussed my concern that as a single parent, I had to leave by 5:00 p.m. sharp each day to pick up my children.

Many times our staff meetings would go beyond this time so I would miss out on the dialogue that occurred after I departed. I was very sensitive to needing to leave — no one else on the team had a time limitation. Welch listened and we worked through how to handle this so that I was involved at the same level as the rest of the leadership team. He made adjustments to the schedule and agendas within the meetings. He taught me how to set limits, delegate and make difficult choices. He coached me through this challenging time, while always holding me accountable to a high standard of performance. We also discussed leadership attributes that I could grow and develop to be seen and heard as a strong leader in the organization. Welch taught me about not only leading my team, but also about being seen as a leader across the broader organization.

My manager took the time to understand the effect of daily life on a member of his leadership team. While he did not get involved in my after-work activities, he did take the time to understand the team dynamic and how it affected my part on the team. That meant a lot to me and played an important role in giving me the tools and confidence to continue to grow in the organization.

This experience taught me about compassion in the face of life changes. I will always be grateful for this experience with Welch because it set an example that stayed with me throughout my career. I knew what it was like to go through difficult personal times and I had an example of how a manager could support me through it. I was still held just as accountable as everyone else on the team, but I felt supported, with dignity and respect, through this time. Throughout my career, I have had many opportunities to display the same example. I call this "Leading with Heart."

Taking the time to understand individuals on your team is even more important when nurturing diversity. By definition, cookie-cutter solutions don't work when everyone brings their own challenges. However, the rewards of crafting individual solutions that employees can use to enhance their contributions to the team will multiply the effectiveness of the entire organization.

Open Leadership

By building on the strengths each member brings to the table, leaders reinforce the unique talents that can contribute to a successful project. When employees are not afraid to express their authentic personalities, the results can be transformational to the group and the bottom line.

> *When employees are not afraid to express their authentic personalities, the results can be transformational to the group and the bottom line.*

Welch demonstrated the power of collective contributions by openly discussing the value of diversity, calling our inclusive mandate a "competitive imperative."

Nelson Mandela, who led South Africa out of apartheid toward a multicultural, integrated society, may have said it best: "A good head and a good heart are always a formidable combination."

By starting with challenging, measurable, well-articulated goals, intertwined with a personal approach to coaching your employees for success, you create a team that both works together and grows individually. That is the foundation for Woven Leadership.

SECTION II: THE WEFT

"This above all: to thine own self be true, and it must follow, as the night the day, thou canst not then be false to any man."
— *William Shakespeare*

CHAPTER 5

CREATIVITY RUNS THROUGH IT

"Creativity is the power to connect the seemingly unconnected."
—*William Plomer (African-born English writer)*

Change is difficult. It requires stepping out of your comfort zone and taking risks. The word "Luddite," which most of us today would consider a derogatory term for those who fail to embrace new technology, was actually coined by weavers in the early 1800s. These artisans resisted the adoption of mechanized looms because they feared it would put them out of business. In fact, British textile makers faced with an industrial revolution that threatened to change their way of life went so far as to burn the wide-framed automated looms that were the centerpiece of new factories popping up in the cities. In the battle of man versus progress, innovation always wins, but that doesn't stop people from digging in their heels as they resist the inevitable. Today, no one wants to be labeled a Luddite, but many workers fear that change could impact their lives in ways they aren't ready to accept.

Change is a necessary ingredient for creativity. The goal of diverse organizations is to break out of the same old pattern and find new methods of innovation. The diverse organization has the ability to bring together unique perspectives that would not otherwise exist. Certainly a strong imperative is necessary to motivate an organization to understand that a change needs to occur. After the HP-COMPAQ merger, I was leading the Service Desk operation in HP's outsourcing and was responsible for driving the merged companies' consolidation and transformation of operations. We had an imperative to be competitive and win new outsourcing opportunities in the market. Without a competitive operation, we would have been unable to make progress. It was a very difficult time due to the fact that the operation had matured in the U.S. and the business model needed to be more competitive. I had to explain to my organization that we could not continue in the current situation because we were losing business. We had to transform our operation to be competitive. Even though the changes were still difficult for the organization, this open dialogue about our business imperative helped employees understand why it was necessary to change.

Once the business realities were laid out for the team, we could work on devising solutions to become more competitive by improving operational efficiency, improving the customer experience and managing employee development. When the organization came together to work on the future model, we would all discuss how to be creative by looking at how other industries drove innovation and then create our own unique solutions. Many times we would invite folks from outside organizations to our business planning sessions to spark new ways of thinking.

Diversity of thought and experience is critical to problem-solving in order to generate new ways of doing business, but unity of purpose is essential.

Diversity of thought and experience is critical to problem-solving in order to generate new ways of doing business, but unity of purpose is essential. This particular team originated from different locations across the Americas, and came together to work on the future plans while also gaining an understanding of each other and their respective cultures. It was important to take time to let the teams and their respective team members get to know one another and understand their unique perspectives. This is a critical step in moving an organization forward. It built the relationships across the teams and the geographies in order to work together on the plans.

At one time I had an employee challenge the organization by pointing out that it was too difficult to work across the geography. The argument was that it would be much easier to create unique plans in each country and not collaborate across the organization. I listened to this feedback and acknowledged the difficulties, but pointed out that if we took the time in the beginning to understand not only the differences but also the similarities, we would find that there are a lot of ways we could leverage our strengths. When you take the time to look at how groups are similar, it helps to build a common understanding and bridges perceived gaps.

Prescription for Change

One of the leading agents of change in the medical field is Dr. Claire Pomeroy. The vice chancellor for Human Health Sciences and dean of the School of Medicine at UC Davis Health System is a fan of disruptive innovation. "You have to innovate at the interfaces of methods and cultures to create true breakthroughs rather than trying to innovate within silos," she says. That requires reaching outside your comfort zone.

Pomeroy's goal is to improve health for all. She recognized early on that the traditional medical delivery models aren't sufficient because they only focus on the 15 percent of health that is attributable to medical care delivery. Social determinants, such as poverty, affect people's well-being more than access to surgery and medications do. Therefore, in order to have an impact, she advocates teaming up with urban planners, sociologists, lawyers and others to fundamentally improve the health of the community she serves.

Even within her organization, Pomeroy strives to attract diverse teams because she believes that is the best way to foster creativity. By bringing together people from different departments, representing different constituencies or from different social and generational backgrounds, she creates opportunities for a well-balanced discussion. Then, she supports the role of a leader to define a shared vision to keep those smart, powerful people in the room until a solution can be crafted, tasks divided up and a new strategy implemented.

Leaders of diverse teams have to answer the "what's in it for me" and the "what's in it for us" question before they can ask all the members to work for the common good.

Creative Rivalry

When crafting new ways of doing business, deciding whom to include at the table is very important. Like President Abraham Lincoln, who famously created a "Team of Rivals" by appointing his opponents to his cabinet when he was elected, creative leaders value constructive dissension.

It is not enough to encourage divergent opinions, you have to listen to them, even when what they are saying is difficult to hear or is offered in a negative way. In my experience, sometimes the cynics are the most valuable voices at a meeting. Over time I have learned to listen to the "squeaky wheel" because it often has a story to tell, a problem to be fixed, or an observation that no one else wants to bring up for fear of retribution. As a leader, if you can encourage productive dissension, you will have a deeper understanding of the issues and challenges within and around your organization.

During my tenure as a global support operations executive at HP, my team was based in many locations around the world. At times, employees on widespread organizational conference calls would speak up loudly about an issue. Sometimes, an employee would be negative, using sarcasm and derogatory comments

Over time I have learned to listen to the "squeaky wheel" because it often has a story to tell, a problem to be fixed, or an observation that no one else wants to bring up for fear of retribution.

to make his or her point. While many leaders would be put off and want the person's direct manager to reprimand and counsel the employee, I was intrigued. I by no means encourage negative behavior or tolerate disrespectful conduct as it can be very harmful to the team; however, I do not automatically discount everything a cynic says. Cynics may well have a point — a poorly expressed one, perhaps, but one shared by others that needs to be addressed.

I often made time to meet with one of these outspoken critics. I would try to understand the cynic's frame of reference. Was this person's perspective limited or shared by the rest of the team? Was the comment valid? Who needed to be empowered to address the situation? I also found that when I took the time to meet one-on-one, I could listen, learn and eventually earn this person's trust. Bringing a cynic over as an ally is a very powerful tactic. Former adversaries can help bridge the gap with other dissenters. I would often call key team members just to ask how it was going. This would be an open dialogue so that I could keep a finger on the pulse of the widespread operation and pick up creative ideas to propel us forward. I did my best to be approachable. I often told my team the only feedback I feared was that which I did not get. Certain people kept me aware of what was going on. I made it a point to call on them to give me feedback on morale and what could be done to improve the organization. It was often harsh criticism, but I always thanked them.

It's important to create an environment where ideas can be debated. While cynicism isn't healthy as a group norm, you do want some dissension among your team when it comes to bringing out different perspectives and ideas. Disagreement and debate are productive means of fostering new ideas. Many times it's the outlier's perspective that brings in a creative way of looking at a problem.

Safe Haven

Creativity grows when it is nurtured in a safe environment where it can take root and put out some tentative leaves before it might be pummeled by the harsh realities of the business world.

Dr. Pomeroy of UC Davis understands that true leaders build a framework that brings out the best in everyone regardless of background by establishing a safe environment that nurtures and encourages each member to speak up and contribute in his or her own way. Creative meetings start by making sure all possible points of view have a place at the table. If you are coming up with a technology fix, don't just have technicians in the room. If you bring in the customer care and sales people, you may find solutions that work for everyone. Diversity of opinion results in an abundance of options for creating innovation.

> *Diversity of opinion results in an abundance of options for creating innovation.*

By building a safe environment where any crazy idea can be put on the table, you increase your chances for success. Some ideas will actually be crazy, but their value will be to open a new way of looking at a problem that leads to a valid idea.

Creative Jam

Who brings up the idea should be less important than the concept itself. Some people are naturally shy about speaking up at meetings. That is where a history of embracing input from all sources can make a big difference.

A former colleague and executive in the IT outsourcing business, Robert Farrell, was a master at getting people to riff off ideas in meetings. Like jazz musicians, they would play with a strategy, exploring new angles, adding other aspects, stressing new tactics, until they hit on a workable idea. His secret? How you handle the first person to bring forward a new idea will determine how many ideas follow.

He didn't penalize people for suggesting an untried note. He knew this method would result in some wrong turns. By definition, a new idea will have a greater likelihood of being "wrong" because there is not an established path to success. Therefore, the consequences of being wrong need to be in proportion to the payoff of a big "right."

Still, Farrell warned, when I asked him about his innovative style, that brainstorming is a delicate balance. You don't want to create chaos or break any laws. "It can't be a romp through the forest," he said.

Diversity leadership requires a commitment to running inclusive meetings and giving honest feedback. Only in a safe environment where everyone's views are valued can creative brainstorming thrive.

In today's fast-paced business world, leaders have to be able to quickly adopt new strategies. You have to be meticulous, but not a perfectionist. To return to our weaving analogy, Navajo weavers would intentionally leave a mistake in each rug because they believed only God is perfect. Sometimes in business, we have to go with the solution that works, even if it is not perfect, and then adjust as we move forward toward the goal. This is a very effective way to keep moving fast. If you wait for a finely crafted masterpiece, you may ultimately miss the market opportunity. Getting a new idea out as a trial run and learning along the way will help in the process of finding the right solution.

Creativity and diversity go hand in hand. People from different backgrounds approach a problem with different perspectives. "That is not an obstacle; it is an asset," was how Farrell looked at it. Because of that inclusive philosophy, he was successful in global outreach efforts to build innovative solutions.

Global Imperative

The world is changing. The task for a successful organization is to find a way to get a customer to yes. Most interactions with fellow team members, departments or clients, however, do not involve simple negotiations. There can be complexities that require consideration of many gradients in between. That is where creativity comes into play. What factors can be brought to bear that were not considered before? An organization empowered to think in new ways can often find more ways to get to a creative solution than an organization with only a few tried and true options in its toolbox.

Plus, it is a lot more fun for everyone to be involved in creating new solutions. Take the time to work with customers on new ideas rather than focusing only on internal discussions for the new ideas. While this seems

When your employees are involved in creating the future solutions, they will be more invested in the success of those solutions.

like an obvious course of action, many times an organization thinks they already know what the customer wants. Taking the time to do a focus group or survey of what your customers are struggling with could open up whole new options that would have otherwise been impossible to generate without asking those customers. Likewise, when your employees are involved in creating the future solutions, they will be more invested in the success of those solutions. This will create a stronger outcome and a loyal organization that wants to be around to celebrate the victory.

An effective way to bring creativity to the forefront of an organization is to ask yourself the question "How would we do this if we were just starting this business?" Many times the complexities of the current, possibly dysfunctional, state of working immobilize the creative thinking process and make it stagnant. It can be difficult to create a new way when moving from the current state seems insurmountable to those who have been involved for a long period of time.

One of the major initiatives that I drove at HP was to decrease the operating cost by improving the efficiencies of the commercial support operation. I led the initiative from a perspective of defining a competitive operation regardless of our current situation, and then created a plan to meet it. Innovation resulted from setting aside the current environment and considering what best practices would be if we were just starting, with the benefit of the knowledge of the current competitive landscape. The result was a new design that was not held back by established ways of doing business. We analyzed the gaps between the current operation and the new design, and then created plans to close them. There were many complexities in driving standard ways of doing the operation globally. And there were just as many complexities in looking at the many different cultures across the world to drive the change. Complex change takes time and it takes creativity to be open to changing the current state of business to a new innovative position.

In any change, there are three aspects that must be managed: people, process and technology. With process and technology you can be analytical and decisive. You may debate the most efficient processes or advanced technologies, but it can be broken down and decided through data analysis. The real challenge comes on the people side of the change. I have been stressing the value of diversity in coming up with creative solutions. When you have a diverse team, you have many perspectives to draw from, creates a wider array of choices to consider. On the challenge side of this scenario, bringing together the diverse groups to execute a change requires understanding the impacts from a different perspective.

I spent a lot of time traveling to various parts of the world to review strategies. My goal was to understand the challenges of implementation by understanding the employees' perspectives. A new process could elicit different concerns in Australia than it did in Germany or Brazil. Cultural norms are very real and need to be considered. Many times, the problem is not the solution itself but the way in which it is implemented. For instance, some cultures are very direct during their business conversations and are willing to quickly debate and decide the plans going forward. Others need to have meetings to discuss the change in detail and understand all of the considerations and analysis that led to the plan in order to internalize the change. These disparities can sometimes immobilize an organization because they appear insurmountable. Taking the time to understand how to bridge gaps between cultural divides is imperative to the success of the

Taking the time to understand how to bridge gaps between cultural divides is imperative to the success of the business objectives.

business objectives. Diversity needs to be managed throughout this process from all aspects of the organization and its people involved in the change.

It took creativity and open thinking from every diverse perspective to build and execute a plan to be successful. The results created a very competitive position that would not have been possible without the whole team coming together to build the new operating model.

"The future requires that we think in complex, holistic ways," Dr. Pomeroy of UC Davis believes. That view was not always initially embraced by some of her colleagues in the medical field. They had a strictly defined view of their jobs: to diagnose and treat people who came to them in the clinic or hospital. She was telling them that they had to fundamentally change the way they viewed their world, to think more broadly. That can be overwhelming without a confident leader to show the way.

We must understand that it is pointless to cling to the old ways of doing business —just like in the 1800s, when the automated looms were going to come no matter how much the old guard resisted. Those who invested in the new way of making fabric on a grand scale became part of a lucrative industry. Those who resisted ultimately lost their business.

CHAPTER 6

THE ADAPTABLE TEAM

"Change is the law of life and those who look only to the past or present are certain to miss the future." —*John F. Kennedy*

Like weaving, building a dynamic organization that can adapt to ever-changing business environments takes planning. You can't jump around; you have to have a plan to get to your desired outcome. What makes a team adaptable? Certainly, a strong foundation is essential. Investing the time to develop individuals will help drive the overall performance of the organization and enable the team to adapt as changes occur. The result is an enhanced organization that can capitalize on changes in economic cycles to be more successful.

Growing Up with Change

Some people are more comfortable with change than others. Taking an organization or situation from one state and transforming it to another — whether it is business, personal or making the world a better place— that is what I truly enjoy, what I thrive on. It comes from my childhood. As I mentioned earlier, my father is a retired admiral from the Navy. We were a typical military family: by the time I was 12 years old I had lived in 11 different residences across multiple states. This experience taught me to be resilient. I was constantly introduced to new schools and had to learn over and over again to make new friends. I never had the comfort of the same house in the same neighborhood with the same friends. In fact, by the time we got settled and got to know our new community, it seemed we were then ready for the next adventure. My two sisters and I did not spend any energy complaining or asking my parents why, we just began packing and saying good-bye to our friends. I learned to be adaptable to ever-changing surroundings. At the time I didn't realize the impact it would have on my life as I grew older; it was simply what we did. I've found as I reflect back that I have always been at ease with uprooting and moving from one place to the next. There is a bit of nomadic spirit that I carry with me. When faced with a new situation, I immediately begin to assess how I will adapt. Change energizes me with that same sense of adventure that was my companion growing up.

With all of this behind me, I easily adapted to a transient lifestyle as an executive leading a global operation. My travel schedule was very intense, and I constantly moved about the world holding reviews and working on strategies and plans to move my organization forward. Many times people would ask me how I could go from one time zone to another so easily. They wanted to know if it was difficult being in so many different hotels and locations each month. The travel was never a problem — I adapted to my surroundings just as I had learned to do growing up. I especially looked forward to trips when I was going somewhere I had never been before. This was always, and still is, very exciting for me. It would be a chance to meet new people, learn a new culture and see a part of the world I had yet to explore.

Change as a Process

Although I have learned to be comfortable with change, it is not always the same for others. Many people struggle with workplace transformation and reorganization.

Individuals often hold on to the belief that "they can't let me go; my work is too important." They may not see any way to do business other than the way it is being done now. This tunnel vision can make it difficult to understand the big picture. People become attached to their jobs. However, this dedication can limit an organization when single-minded employees are asked to shift to a new role.

Leaders can help the transition by always stressing the importance of being adaptable. When employees develop a wide range of skills along the course of a career, they are better prepared with options when change comes. They develop into a valuable asset and have wider options.

Taking the time to expand skills and leadership qualities creates the ability to adapt during challenging business climates.

While I was driving transformation at HP, jobs would sometimes be eliminated as efficiencies were implemented into the business processes. Many times employees were asked to switch to entirely different jobs, where they were needed. Taking the time to expand skills and leadership qualities creates the ability to adapt during challenging business climates.

Change is a process. As with physical grief, each person moves through the emotions associated with change at his or her own pace. Some will skip some stages, lingering in others, or move back and forth. As a leader, you need to understand that this is human nature and to be compassionate about what they are

going through. At the same time you need to be realistic that if
you don't take care of the business imperative to be competitive,
everyone's job will be in jeopardy.

Taking the time to hear an employee can make a big
difference in how news is processed. As a team leader, you have
the opportunity to lead your team through dark periods to a
brighter future.

Willing to Adapt

Business environments are constantly changing. Certainly,
technology changes quickly and the only way to keep up is to
continue to grow your knowledge and skills. In today's world,
a company can't keep doing the same thing and continue to
succeed. If you don't evolve, you get left behind. This philosophy
sets the stage for a mindset that is always looking for better ways
to do things.

Remember COBOL? That was how I started in HP, writing
computer programs in COBOL. But I was soon faced with an
industry that was starting to move away from COBOL as the
primary business programming language. I took the initiative and
started transitioning to network engineering to ensure that I had a
relevant skill for years to come. Although COBOL programmers
were in demand for a long time after I decided to switch gears, it
was a good decision for me to continue to adapt in the changing
technology industry. I took this initiative on my own, knowing
that I would be more valuable in my career if I learned different
areas of Information Technology. I took classes to learn more
about telecommunications and networking technologies. I was at
the forefront of the Internet as I installed the connection from the
HP facility where I worked to the World Wide Web. Without the

change from an application programmer to network engineer I would have missed out on an exciting time in the IT industry. This detour in my career ended up being instrumental in positioning me for a future opportunity to run the Telecommunication department for the facility where I worked. Sometimes a change seems small and insignificant, but in the long run can be a key building block to a future opportunity.

Preparing Yourself for the Future

The explicit message from management has to be an imperative to constantly grow personally and professionally. If this goal is endorsed at all levels, then employees will grow into the leaders your organization will need in the future. As a leader, you need to encourage growth in your employees. Annually, I sat down with each member of my staff to review their accomplishments against their goals for the past year and set the coming year's goals. I would always take the time to ask each of them, "What's your next step or goal? What do you want to learn in the coming year?" I would assure them that I wasn't trying to imply they leave, but I was simply encouraging them to think about future goals so that I could give them opportunities to develop skills. As an example, I might have an operations manager who has a desire to work in HR in the future. I would give him or her the role of liaison to HR and have that person work on employee morale projects during the year.

> *The explicit message from management has to be an imperative to constantly grow personally and professionally.*

I would strive to facilitate different opportunities for each person based on his or her personal goals. This gave employees a chance to develop and build relationships in areas that may have opportunities in the future. Sometimes I would talk to someone who said he or she was really happy with his or her position in the company, and did not see changing roles for at least a couple years. That was fine too; we could then discuss skill building in the current role or leadership opportunities within the role. The important point is to encourage team members to be adaptable by gaining new skills and taking on challenging opportunities to grow and develop.

Leaders also have to walk the talk. Personally, I was constantly learning and growing. One of the most profound growth opportunities that I had was with the Accelerated Development Program. Each year HP would pick high-potential managers to participate in intensive leadership training to propel them to higher-level executive positions. I was chosen into this leadership program in 2000. The combination of mentoring, executive coaching and enrollment in an executive training course at University of Pennsylvania, Wharton School of Business Executive Development Program, was a life-changing experience for me. The two-week mini-MBA course consists of topical lectures, business simulation and organizational effectiveness. The course included candid feedback from the group, an experience that proved insightful, humbling and empowering all at once. It revealed the areas where I needed work and helped me capitalize on my strengths.

Prior to taking the course, I had been asked to take on a new role at HP. It was a promotion to lead a larger organization. At first, I was hesitant. However, after my training, I came back and committed to the new role. I found I was more direct, more strategic and more effective at holding people accountable. My employees, my peers and my boss all noticed — in a good way. That is the power of focusing on your development to be prepared for new opportunities. As difficult as it can be to find the time to invest in training, the right program can advance your career — and your organization — by years.

Later in my career, after leading the global Enterprise Service Desk outsourcing operation, I approached my manager and his manager to discuss what steps I would need to take to be considered for a vice president role at HP. I was told I would need to take on a new role that included aspects of the VP role that I aspired to and be seen as a leader that could grow into the next level. I was encouraged to learn as much as I could about this new area during the coming year and build as many relationships as possible across the organization so that when the time came, I would be known and my leadership skills would be apparent. When the year was up and the new opportunity became available, I was ready. I competed for the position and was selected. The lesson here is to make it known that you have aspirations and to be willing to change what you are doing to gain the skills necessary. This will make you more adaptable to new opportunities and more valuable to the overall organization.

> *The lesson here is to make it known that you have aspirations and to be willing to change what you are doing to gain the skills necessary.*

Unexpected Opportunities

Change, although not always easy, often brings opportunities. My friend Marco Rodriguez is proof that true leaders can find inspiration in adversity. Although he was left wheelchair-bound after a serious car accident 15 years ago, he has gone on to accomplish more than many able-bodied people. Today, he serves on the board of the Sacramento State Alumni Association, is president of the Board of the Mexican Cultural Center of Northern California, is a member of American Leadership Forum and is past chairman of the Board of the Sacramento Hispanic Chamber of Commerce. He served on the National Council on Disabilities, advising President George W. Bush, and is now a gubernatorial appointee to the State Independent Living Council.

After Rodriguez' car rolled four times on an icy road in the middle of the Mexican desert, he was stranded with a broken back. Luckily, a family and a man with one of the few mobile phones in the area at the time stopped, and through friends of friends arranged for him to be flown to a hospital hours away. The rehabilitation process was long and painful as Rodriguez, a senior financial representative for Principal Financial Group, adjusted to life without the use of his legs. His love for his wife and young son who survived the accident with minor scratches and bruises, made him feel blessed. "I am very lucky," he tells people. While he didn't have to go back to work for financial reasons, his clients encouraged him to return to his advisory position and he soon found a renewed sense of purpose, ranking in the top 2 percent of financial advisors nationally.

Mexican immigrant Rodriguez doesn't self-identify solely as Hispanic or disabled, or any other label for that matter. He sees himself and others as more complicated than that. He applies that same inclusive mentality to his hiring decisions on boards and as the leader of his team. "I hire the best person for the job then celebrate all their unique qualities," Rodriguez says.

The active nonprofit volunteer does believe in leveraging targeted resources to accomplish bigger goals. One cause he has worked on is the Mexican Cultural Center Together 200 Years project. It celebrates the shared culinary history and economy of

Mexico and California by bringing gourmet goods manufactured in small rural Mexican towns to Sacramento as part of a series of events centered on the bicentennial celebrations. By bringing people with common interests together, Rodriguez is changing the world. He is creating jobs for micro and women-owned businesses in small Mexican towns and helping Sacramento businesses like the Sacramento River Cats baseball team connect with an important part of their customer base.

Rodriguez didn't have a choice about the physical change he underwent. But he did have a choice in how he reacted to it. "I could have become depressed and die or come through it and impact more people," Rodriguez says. Rodriguez chose to adapt and in the process has become an inspirational example of thriving through adversity.

Change for the Better

If change is so difficult, why do it? Change is the lever that takes a company from surviving (or not) to thriving. And the better a company does, the better its employees' prospects for individual career growth. Throughout my career in the IT industry I have thrived in the constantly changing environment. At one point, I was promoted to a site IT manager role, but before the ink was dry on my business cards, the role was eliminated. In preparing for that job, I had worked on many skills, including managing every aspect of the IT area: customer support, telecommunications and

Change is the lever that takes a company from surviving (or not) to thriving. And the better a company does, the better its employees' prospects for individual career growth.

networking, system management and data center, and PC and Unix engineering. The good news was that when the job I aspired to was eliminated, I had all of those experiences to draw on for a new opportunity. The position to lead customer support distributed across North America and Latin America for HP's internal IT became available. It was a wonderful opportunity at that time in my career. I had been flexible enough to learn new areas and change jobs every couple of years until I rotated through every area of IT. I knew that I needed the variety of skills to be ready for new opportunities. This experience across multiple disciplines helped me throughout my career. It helped me to be adaptable.

I encouraged my staff to continue to rotate and take on new roles. It was a win-win. They gained skills that prepared them for new opportunities and the company enjoyed the flexibility afforded by adaptable employees. I was often able to tackle new strategic initiatives because my team had skills that reached beyond our current scope. Change is dynamic: it provides opportunities for individuals and creates an organization that can roll with the changes.

As far back as the 1940s, legendary leadership guru Peter F. Drucker was advising companies that the only thing certain about the future was that "it holds profound and unpredictable change."[2] He was so right. But I would add that it also holds profound and unpredictable opportunities for individuals and organizations willing to go out and create them.

Change at the Top

Changing team members can bring new resources to a group, but rotating leaders can be an even more powerful way to ensure a dynamic and flexible organization.

Bob Farrell, who I mentioned earlier, was thrust into a high-pressure position from another technology company with a completely different culture. Sometimes that was an impediment because he didn't understand the communication style or history behind why things were done the way they were. But it was also an advantage. Because he didn't know the usual way of rolling out a service or asking another team to collaborate, he was willing to break the unspoken rules. More often than not, that resulted in getting things done. "I was an outsider; I had permission to break the rules because I didn't know them," Farrell explained.

Employees can get too comfortable with a boss. They fall into an easy groove that results in less risk-taking, less creative problem-solving. A true leader constantly challenges team members to try new things, but can only teach them so much. Bringing in new leaders infuses new learning opportunities in a group en masse.

Allowing leaders to move from team to team has the positive effect of exposing them to different aspects of the business. That way, as they move up the organization chart, they can better understand the people and groups they are leading. So mix it up. It's good for the team and the leaders.

Learning, growing and changing, these are more than dream team wish lists. They are requirements for organizations that want to grow and prosper. A good leader both encourages and models an insatiable thirst for new ideas. As Mahatma Gandhi said, "Adaptability is not imitation. It means power of resistance and assimilation."

CHAPTER 7

THE AUTHENTIC LEADER

"You are total. You are full. You have all that you need. Do not underestimate yourself." —spiritual leader Sri Sri Ravi Shankar

The cumulative effect of candidly leading with heart is that you become an authentic — and therefore more effective — leader. All the topics we have talked about so far have been strands in a larger integrated leadership approach that requires being true to yourself and your organization at all times.

I have spent a great deal of time in India for business and pleasure. On an extended visit, I spent time at the Art of Living Foundation, an ashram led by spiritual leader Sri Sri Ravi Shankar. The Foundation engages in a wide array of educational and humanitarian programs that uplift individuals, make a difference in local communities, and foster global change. Art of Living also offers courses focused on breathing, meditation and yoga to assist in alleviating stress, gaining insight and exercising the body.

I learned a great deal about myself, including the fact that I need a cushioned mat if I am going to spend hours sitting cross-legged on the floor. Who knew sitting could be so exhausting! One of the revelations came in the recognition that often when I set out to do something that seems simple, I find, when I am immersed in it, that it is not so simple after all.

Part of the advanced Art of Living course includes silent meditation for more than two days. I found this very challenging. When someone would talk to me, I would instinctively want to respond — sometimes I would open my mouth without even thinking and then catch myself. What ended up being profound during this silence was that outside interactions ceased, but the dialogue in my mind carried on. I gained clarity simply because when I went quiet on the outside, it gave me the space and time for my inner thoughts to develop and grow.

As I begin this topic of authenticity, it is appropriate to begin with the idea of self. Knowing who you are, what is important to you and how you want to show up in the world is the first step in the journey of becoming your authentic self.

For me, it was the silence that brought on the deepest learning during the ashram stay. Why? Because it highlighted the fact that I don't need to talk to understand others or have them understand me. When you are practicing silence, you perceive so many things that you would not otherwise notice when you are in the habit of talking. Silence forces you to listen — not only to others but to yourself.

> *More damage has been done by leaders who pretend that they know more than they do and then try to cover up for that ignorance than a thousand "I don't know, let's find out" responses.*

Listening is so obvious, yet so many people have difficulty practicing it. By recognizing the business and social imperative of bringing together people of all races, genders, sexual orientation and business styles you are owning up to the fact that you don't have all the answers. I once heard that you have to embrace your ignorance; only then can you allow yourself to ask the questions that get the unexpected answers.

More damage has been done by leaders who pretend that they know more than they do and then try to cover up for that ignorance than a thousand "I don't know, let's find out" responses.

Only by acknowledging that you rely on the smart, diverse team around you to get the best answers can you productively move on to embrace new ideas. By opening the discussion, you also allow others to admit that they rely on the power of the team to be their most productive.

This open leadership approach builds on itself. Word will get out that you are a leader who values the contributions of the team and you will attract the best and brightest in the organization — and the world. When you are open and authentic, you become a magnet for top talent and creativity.

Studies have shown that what makes most employees happy at work is feeling that they are contributing. Employee satisfaction is not all about money, corner offices or long vacations. Instead, the most-sought-after benefit is a chance to make a

> *When you are open and authentic, you become a magnet for top talent and creativity.*

difference. Think about what motivates you and you may better understand the appeal of this results-based approach.

As a leader you could make it look like you are the ultimate contributor. You could control both the discussion and the output. However, then you would be stifling your team. At times I heard people in my organization say, "Is this what you are looking for?" or "We're trying to figure out what you want." These comments threw out red flags for me and I would abruptly stop the conversation. I let my team know in no uncertain terms that I was asking for ideas and contributions because only the collective knowledge of the team produces the best solution.

I surround myself with a diverse, creative team and unleash them to discover innovative, unique ideas. The team needs to know that I am there to support them in this process, not impede the process. This is done by listening and letting them know that I value their perspectives and opinions. Only by allowing your team to have meaningful impact, thus minimizing your contribution to the discussion but maximizing the power of the solution, do you empower those around you to give their best. By being an authentic, listening leader, you are allowing them to do the same.

Building Authenticity

We are all unique. A true leader celebrates that uniqueness by drawing on the resources each person brings to the table. Instead of forcing conformity, we need to celebrate and capitalize on those differences. If we try to standardize our team members, then we are not allowing them to express their authentic selves and we are cheating the organization of valuable assets.

I often talk about how important it is to be yourself, to be true to your own personal style. A caution here: this does not mean that you act or dress inappropriately for a particular setting. There is a difference between conformity and appropriateness. While I don't believe you need to conform to a group norm, I also don't believe in being disrespectful of the business setting. Sometimes being sensitive to a particular culture is subtle and other times the outward appearance is glaring. While working at HP and leading the outsourcing operation for our customer's internal support, Microsoft was a major customer. When Microsoft would come to meet, their attire often reflected the outdoor, casual roots of the Seattle company. We knew when hosting Microsoft that it was not time to pull out the navy blue banker suit. I would dress appropriately to meet this client, but my style was to wear, at a minimum, a blazer. I would pay attention to what was respectful to the client while also maintaining my own unique, personal style.

Other times, being authentic requires opening up about your personal life situation. I've mentioned that early in my management career I became a single parent. This was one of the most challenging times in my life, but it was also filled with tremendous growth. At work I was the only manager on our team who did not have a spouse helping with children at home. I was tied to a schedule that revolved around dropping kids off at day care in the morning and picking them up by a certain time to meet the day care requirements. Many times meetings would go longer than planned and I would have to excuse myself to pick up my kids on time. This was a difficult situation because I felt I was missing important discussions and decisions. But it also brought a mixed blessing — it forced me to have the discipline to set boundaries and adhere to them. It positioned my children as a priority. I was a manager, but I was also a single parent with full responsibility for my kids during the week. I didn't try to hide this or fade back from my family situation. It was simply part of who I was at that time in my career. At times, when I had to work on the weekends, I would bring my kids into the office with me. They quickly learned where the best candy jars were located and how to make hot chocolate at the coffee station. I would set them up to color on the white board in my office, then when I'd come in to work the following Monday I would have the sweet memory of their presence as the work week began.

Although life was challenging as a single mom, it was part of my journey. I often told my team "family first" and because I held this value with my family, it gave them permission to do the same.

I learned an important lesson about being true to my ideals from Dr. Amerish "Ami" Bera, a county chief medical officer and medical school dean who tried his hand at politics by running for a congressional seat. He shared his very personal story with me and others during his campaign. As a first generation Indian-American, the youngest of three boys, his parents had certain expectations about who he would marry and how he would live. When he married a woman outside the culture, an African-American woman, his parents threatened to disown him. His mother even accused him of bringing shame on the family and threatened to commit suicide. "That sent me inward," he said. The young couple spent a lot of time examining their bond in a way many couples never take the time to verbalize. "I had to make a choice," Ami said. "I could give in to my parents and reject my love, but then I would have to live with the knowledge of what I had done for the rest of my life." Instead, this introspective young man came to understand that his parents' reactions were coming from a place of fear. They were afraid of going outside the traditions they knew and understood. They were afraid of losing the only way of life they knew. By meeting their objections with compassion and love instead of anger, Ami and his now-wife not only earned a grudging acceptance, she has won over her in-laws as a favored daughter-in-law. "My mother talks to my wife more than she does me," Ami said recently with a laugh.

Authenticity at the Center

In order to be truly authentic, you have to be completely honest with your team. That means telling all of the truth with no spin. "Need-to-know" communication results in fewer people being provided with enough information to make informed decisions — always an inferior business position.

This is true on a business and personal level. I will tell you that I struggled over the years with how much of my life to bring to work each day. At first, I felt that I had to downplay my life outside the office in order to look dedicated. Although I would talk to my coworkers about my weekend or various things going on in my life, I was careful about how much I shared.

I learned quickly, however, that managing people was not just about the business at hand, it was also about the people themselves. I was interacting with complex individuals who had hopes and dreams and struggles. By connecting on a personal level, I could be more effective at leading a team to reach our shared business goals.

One of the people who taught me this important lesson was the dean of the UC Davis School of Medicine, Dr. Claire Pomeroy. I have mentioned her before, as she is one of the most accomplished people I know. She is an expert in infectious diseases and a professor of internal medicine and microbiology and immunology. She is leading her 8,000 employees into a brave new future that emphasizes social responsibility. She led the way on National Institute of Health and National Science Foundation programs to address disparities in gender medicine, but for years she did not disclose a very formative time in her life, concerned that it might hurt her image in the eyes of peers and employees alike. The personal story she held inside for years was that she grew up in foster care. It was only recently that she started to talk about her childhood and what she had to overcome. She confided to me that at first she was very hesitant to talk. However, the reaction from those who heard her story was eye-opening. When she let down her guard and allowed herself to appear vulnerable, it gave others the courage to share their stories. "I was able to connect with people in a new way and be more effective," she told me.

People do not only learn by hearing about success stories. They learn when they understand the common challenges faced by others and how they were able to overcome.

How much to share depends on the organization culture and local customs. You need to maintain a sense of propriety for your position, but that doesn't mean you have to be a leadership machine. The more authentic you are with those around you about who you are, what motivates you and how you would like to contribute, the more effective you will be. At the bottom line, diversity leadership is all about building a more effective organization by valuing all the uniqueness that individuals possess—and embracing your own uniqueness.

Diversity PRIDE

One of the most powerful lessons I've learned about being true to myself was while serving on the HP PRIDE Executive Advisory Board. I consider myself an ally to the LGBT community, which means that I openly support the rights of lesbian, gay, bisexual, and transgender people. As an executive, I was asked to serve on the advisory council representing my business group at HP. Some colleagues asked, "Why would you take the time to serve if you are not part of that community?" or worse, "What if someone thinks you are part of that community?" These questions never crossed my mind when I was asked to serve and accepted the position on the Executive Advisory Board. My intention was to do my best to understand and support the equality and opportunities of this group of employees. I had also been involved in mentoring and supporting many other kinds of employee groups throughout my HP career.

My participation was part of a journey of learning by truly listening to the employees that were part of HP PRIDE. When I traveled to various locations, I would have lunch meetings with folks from the local HP PRIDE group and ask them what challenges they faced in the workplace and in life. I did not assume that I knew the answer even though I had friends, family and colleagues who were part of the LGBT community. Instead, I focused on truly listening. It paid off in a deeper understanding of each person's individual experience.

The biggest lesson came when I was asked to go to the annual Out & Equal Workplace Summit. It was there that I listened, observed and learned. I was the minority in the mix, one of only a few straight people attending the conference. I learned what transgender means and what it's like to go through the transition because of the refreshing openness and honesty of those willing to tell me their stories. Everyone was kind and willing to share their experiences so I could really understand their daily challenges. As the conference progressed, I found that I was accepted and welcomed by everyone. It was humbling.

I had been asked to attend the conference to accept an award and give a speech on behalf of HP. I was very honored to take on this role. When I went to the podium to give my prepared speech, I had a sudden urge to do more, to speak from my heart. "I have often said that I am not part of the LGBT community," I admitted. "Yet after being here over the past few days, as an ally, I feel I am part of the community. ..." I said this with as much gratitude as I could convey. That observation received a big round of applause that took me by surprise.

What I realized is that instead of highlighting all of the differences and separating myself, I began to see the similarities. Each person, gay, straight, black, white, male or female is made up of multiple dimensions. The best way to relate to others is to find facets we share. I am a woman who has been discriminated against and isolated at various times in my life and career. I had been a single mother who struggled and was judged by others along the way. Being involved in the LGBT community as an ally has taught me more about being myself and celebrating who I am than almost any other situation. I relished this experience during my time at HP. I became involved to serve others and ended up benefiting from the experience myself far beyond what I ever could have imagined.

> *Each person, gay, straight, black, white, male or female is made up of multiple dimensions.*

Effective teams need passion. Compartmentalizing yourself limits passion, thereby limiting effectiveness. Being open about your background, experiences and life outside of work makes you a strong leader, a more authentic leader.

Revealing a little about yourself at work can have real benefits. You make connections with people in ways that forge a common ground. A sense of openness gives you credibility as a leader and a person. I was often told by my staff, after I had an opportunity to meet with employees while traveling to various operation centers, they would get feedback that, "Kim seems so normal, so down to earth. She's approachable and open." This would clear the way so people could bring forward issues to be solved in a positive way. I found this to be invaluable to the health of the organization.

Accountable Authenticity

While authenticity may seem to be a nebulous, "touchy-feely" concept, accountability is actually one of the best ways to inject your true priorities into your day-to-day activities. If something is important to you — bringing more diversity into the organization, doing a better job of connecting with customers, cutting costs or increasing sales — you can qualify it, but it becomes more powerful if you quantify it. Putting numbers to your vision and mission gives them added value. It also gives your team an incentive to make them a reality. You still have to explain why the goals are important, how you came to the numbers and help facilitate reaching those goals successfully. But putting a measurement system in place is the first step.

When leading teams around the world there was no way I could micromanage every aspect of their operations; I was not physically in every office with them every day. What I could do instead was inspire these teams to reach specific goals. I set daily, weekly, monthly and quarterly goals and reviewed regularly. It was easy to see if something was getting off track or not making progress so I could put corrective actions in place. While leading the operation delivering outsource services for Enterprise Helpdesk operations, I was in charge of over 250 accounts worldwide. Each month we would review the key metrics for every account. These goals were not arbitrary. They were designed to gauge whether we were delivering on the commitments we had made to these customer accounts. Any

> *If goals are arbitrary, unreachable or a distraction from the true mission of the organization, then people become frustrated, dispirited, and eventually unproductive.*

metrics that were not meeting the threshold levels would have an action plan to get back on track.

We have all seen what happens when leaders aren't honest about what the team can accomplish. If goals are arbitrary, unreachable or a distraction from the true mission of the organization, then people become frustrated, dispirited, and eventually unproductive. Authentic accountability is vital to getting results and equalizing the playing field for everyone.

Authentically Creative

Creativity doesn't thrive in a vacuum. Only by mixing disparate elements often found deep inside ourselves and others do we come up with the wild combinations that make life interesting and audacious goals possible.

Who knew peanut butter and chocolate would taste great together, or that phones and computers would ever merge to make us mobile machines. It takes a lot of self-confidence to take a chance on a new idea and it is imperative to move an organization forward.

You can't take those kinds of risks if you are always trying to cover your tracks, be who someone else wants you to be or read off of an old script handed down from generation to generation. You have to look inside you and do what you think is right. And be prepared to admit if it wasn't the right choice. Creativity requires authenticity.

It also requires you to be self-aware. Whenever I would take responsibility for a new organization, I would set the stage by laying out my philosophies and expectations. One of these would be creativity. I would take the risk of utilizing this word as a way to describe getting new and innovative ideas. The word sometimes gives people the impression of something too "artsy" or nebulous. But I specifically used this word because I wanted to set the tone that we would solve our business problems by considering new, sometimes unconventional ways to get to the breakthroughs that would propel our results forward.

Adapting to the Changing Self

We are all living, growing beings. What works for us today may not be right tomorrow. And what one person considers the opportunity of a lifetime may be too limiting for someone else. That is why it is important to check in with yourself from time to time to see if you are making the highest and best use of your skills. Are there areas where you could improve? What training, mentoring or other experiences do you need to undertake to get where you need to go? Don't be afraid to ask for help from a wide range of people — peers, managers, industry associates. I've learned from many different sources over the years — boards I've served on, mentors and people I've mentored, experiences inside and outside of the workplace. Growth can come where you least expect it, so always be open to that piece of insight that could help you react better in the next difficult situation.

The Authentic You

Over the years I have often thought of my career journey as tangled threads. I would embark on a new opportunity and work hard to learn and grow and then that opportunity would lead me to the next opportunity. I usually had an idea of what I wanted to grow toward and I would make sure I got the experience and training necessary to reach my next goal. There were times when I learned that I didn't have a passion for a particular job and I would take the steps to move to something that I did have passion about.

It is important as a leader to keep learning and growing. It is also important that you cultivate this education priority within your team. My greatest satisfaction came when one of my employees would get promoted into a new opportunity. It was so satisfying to play a positive part in someone's career journey. By growing the individuals, you grow the team and the whole organization. You also help folks to feel valued and motivated in their work.

Authenticity is both the building block for creating diverse, accountable, adaptable and creative teams and the powerful result of taking the time to nurture a culture where people aren't afraid to give their best selves for the sake of the shared organizational goal.

Andrew Cohen, founder of EnlightenNext, a popular business retreat leader, said: "The authentic self is the best part of a human being. It's the part of you that already cares, that is already passionate about evolution. When your authentic self miraculously awakens and becomes stronger than your ego, then you will truly begin to make a difference in this world. You will literally enter into a partnership with the creative principle."[3]

THE FRINGE

"Our life is composed greatly from dreams, from the unconscious, and they must be brought into connection with action. They must be woven together." —Anais Nin

CHAPTER 8

AFTERWORD — LEADING WITH PURPOSE

"What you leave behind is not what is engraved in stone monuments, but what is woven into the lives of others."
—Pericles, Greek statesman (c. 495-429 B.C.)

In Greek mythology, the most powerful characters are the Fates, the three Moerae sisters. These women controlled a man's destiny by weaving the fabric of his life. Clotho, the spinner, wound the thread of life; Lachesis, the measurer, determined how long an individual's life would be; and Atropos, also known as "she who cannot be turned," cut the thread of life when the time came.

The great social science lecturer Joseph Campbell pointed out that while fate may determine when a person dies, what is important is the quality of the journey. Instead of a predetermined, linear life, he preferred to use the Buddhist metaphor of Indra's Net of interconnected gems reflecting off one another. The best way for an individual to play his or her role in this web of life is to "follow your bliss," he often said.[4]

Knock, Knock

There comes a time in almost everyone's life that the world knocks, asking to be addressed. Sometimes it is a gentle, persistent rapping heard during international flights while gazing out the window at the mesmerizing clouds. Sometimes the call comes in the form of a knock on the side of the head when you read a headline or see an injustice that just won't let you turn away. And for others it is a profound personal experience that leaves you a different person with different desires for your life.

Although the situation can manifest in different ways, it demands that you go out and share your passion with people outside the isolated niche that has consumed your universe up to this point in time. Some find ways to answer while continuing their careers. They may serve on boards, volunteer or get involved in causes that they are passionate about.

My shift was a gradual change in my sense of purpose. For all the 29 years I was in the high-tech industry, I thrived on the day-to-day demands of my career. But as I advanced in my career, something changed. I began to seriously reflect on my life. I had always enjoyed the various challenging positions that I had taken on, but a growing part of me had a desire to do something new and different, something more purposeful that would have a real impact on the world beyond my organization. Over time, my vision of a life out of the corporate world became clearer. There was not one moment where I suddenly realized I needed to take a fork in the road to a new destination. It was a series of moments that added up to a point in time that I knew it was time for me to do something new.

> *"There comes a time when you know it is time to do something different. Then it takes courage to make the change."*

My father retired as an admiral at close to the same age that I was when I decided to move on. When I asked him why he decided to leave such an illustrious career in the military he told me, "There comes a time when you know it is time to do something different. Then it takes courage to make the change." I am following a bit in my father's footsteps. As he left his long-term naval career, he got involved in nonprofit work along with various entrepreneurial ventures and consulting opportunities.

I remember when he first told me he had decided to retire early. He was in his early 50s and I wondered what he would do after so many years in the same career. I knew he had hobbies, but I also knew he intended to look into new opportunities. When I began to have a change of heart about continuing my corporate career, I also began to understand what had led my father to his decisions. And I knew he would understand my seemingly sudden decision to move on to a new chapter.

As I began to seriously contemplate shifting into a new chapter, I had a few projects in mind, including writing a book and speaking on leadership focused on diversity and authenticity to help others embrace the philosophies that I am so passionate about. Another project was to start a nonprofit to drive prevention and early intervention of teenage drug and alcohol addiction. Although I had these projects in mind, it was still a major decision filled with more unknowns than knowns. What I did know was that it was time for me to make a change. To stay in my job when I knew in my heart and my head that I wanted to go would have been impossible.

I had always been genuinely enthusiastic about my career. I often told people that I looked forward to work each and every day. I truly enjoyed leading large operational transformations. The people who worked on my staff and throughout the organization made the decision to leave difficult. But, I also often said that if I couldn't get up every day and look forward to what I did, then I would not continue doing it. Although I was still challenged by the work I was doing, I knew I was ready to move on. It was

time to start a new journey that was solely defined and created
by me. And, so, I did. I have never looked back with regret. An
incredible sense of freedom emerges when you accept what is in
your heart and give yourself the permission to flourish in your
own life. My intention was to be in service, to give back, and to
take control of every aspect of my life.

I was fortunate to have other friends and colleagues that had
left the corporate world to start new ventures, and they served as
role models for me. My friend and former colleague at HP, Jyoti
Narula, who runs her own HR consulting business and is a trustee
with World Alliance Youth Empowerment, a nonprofit based out
of the Art of Living Foundation, explained how she came to leave
her corporate career. She was sitting in her office one day looking
out the glass windows. It was raining. She decided to open the
window for the lovely smell of fresh rain and the breeze blowing
mist inside. After a few minutes a man from the maintenance
department told her that she should close her window because
the air conditioning was on. He
was just doing his job. She politely
complied, but it made her think,
"What am I doing with myself?"
The way she tells it, "As I look
back, I always felt that question
was pushing at me, but I always
pushed it back into the realms of
my subconscious mind. Then, I
realized after 17 years of enjoying a good career with some notable
achievements behind me that I was not close to an answer."

> *"Have we forgotten the most important: you, yourself? Only by being yourself can you live all the aspects of your life with truth and honesty."*

The decision to leave was not an easy one for Narula, but she
remembered the words of the very wise man Sri Sri Ravi Shankar,
"We keep thinking we want to do this and we want to do that
... if you really want to, go ahead ... what will happen? The

maximum is that it will not work out." And with that thought in mind, she left to pursue what gave her more happiness. Narula believes that everything has a placeholder in one's life: career, relations, money. But, she asks, "Have we forgotten the most important: you, yourself? Only by being yourself can you live all the aspects of your life with truth and honesty."

Giving Back

Her Majesty Queen Rania Al-Abdullah of Jordan once said, "I just wake up and feel like a regular person. At the end of the day you are living your life for the people that you represent. It's an honour and a privilege to have that chance to make a difference — a qualitative difference in people's lives — and it's my responsibility to make the most out of that opportunity."[5]

Serving is an honor and a responsibility. Although I was not royalty, I'd like to think that I made a difference in some of the lives I touched while in my corporate career. I certainly had opportunity to coach, mentor and inspire many people with my broad responsibilities over the years. I took this role very seriously and enjoyed it immensely when I saw one of my employees grow and thrive along his or her journey. Yet, there was a yearning to be more purposeful and effect change beyond my corporate reach. I wanted to take my well-developed leadership skills and apply them to community service and endeavors with a purpose.

I had a lot of great role models to guide my career with a purpose. One of my managers, Larry Welch, pointed out that the nonprofit world needed more diverse voices. People passionate about a cause decide to join the cause because they believe in the work. These dedicated individuals joined together with diverse backgrounds and skills make a powerful combination to help change the world. Welch made the point, "There is a great opportunity for people from the for-profit world to be in service to nonprofits to help them be successful by including a wide range of perspectives." Those words inspired me to share the skills I had learned in my job with causes that could make a difference.

It's never to early or too late to follow your passion. One woman who learned early that she wanted to do meaningful work is Wendy Beecham, CEO of Watermark, an organization that connects exceptional women leaders to enable them to enhance their impact. Beecham worked around the world in high-profile, high-pressure jobs implementing digital publishing initiatives and managing change in organizations such as Thomson and LexisNexis. After being named managing director of a UK division of Thomson by the age of 43, she found herself back in the United States looking for more stability in her life. "I had achieved a high level of success and responsibility early in my career," she recalls. "But the level of intensity was affecting my health and I wanted to put down roots."

> *It's never to early or too late to follow your passion.*

Beecham made the decision to quit with no fallback plan. "I had to remove myself so that I could truly create a different future for myself; I had to walk away from the trappings of success that keep you tethered," she recalls. After a stint consulting with CEOs, she discovered the nonprofit group Forum for Women Entrepreneurs/ Executives (recently re-named Watermark). The board was looking for someone who had been a former CEO and could take on a transformational operational role, and she was looking for someplace she could have a lasting impact. It was a perfect fit. She took the organization through an entire strategy and re-branding process and recently announced the birth of

Watermark to symbolize the impact women have on each other and the world.

One of the tools Beecham brought to her new career was the inclusiveness that had helped her be successful in her previous life shaking up staid organizations to position them for future growth. She had always been intentional about bringing in large candidate pools for each position and then objectively choosing the best candidate. She looked for fresh skill sets, thoughts and styles. "Often I would be surprised about who the best person turned out to be when the interview process was over," she says. She maintains that same open mind when she is hiring for Watermark. "Just because it is an organization for women, I don't hesitate to interview male candidates for jobs," she says.

Able-Minded

Another longtime inspiration is fellow leader Mike Ziegler. This is a man who had a successful career leading, owning and selling large retail operations. By chance, he happened to walk in the door of a small nonprofit called Placer Rehabilitation Industries. "It was a typical nonprofit," Ziegler recalls. "The leaders had no focus on business." Instead, they were driven by a desire to create jobs for disabled people. "I realized I could use the skills I had used to make money to help them do this very important work and it changed my life."

Ziegler soon joined as president, CEO and chief cheerleader. In 25 years, he took the nonprofit from 65 employees and a $250,000 budget to a business solutions provider employing 4,300 people (most with disabilities) and earning more than $150 million in revenues. The company went from an organization dependent on federal and state support to a self-sufficient business serving

Fortune 500 companies and creating opportunities for one of the most disenfranchised groups in the job market.

"When I am successful, someone's life changes; that is powerful," Ziegler says with his characteristic passion. That is what I call putting your hard-earned business skills to work for a higher cause.

On the international stage, super-celebrity Oprah Winfrey truly understands the importance of giving back. Born in Kosciusko, Mississippi, the future daytime television diva lived alternately with her grandparents, mother and finally, her father in Nashville. At age 17 she began her career at a radio station before going to Tennessee State University to study speech communications and performing arts. She was soon hosting her own television show called "People Are Talking." In 1985, she moved to Chicago to host what became "The Oprah Winfrey Show" and almost immediately began accumulating Emmy Awards.

Oprah has used her celebrity platform and fortune to help others without a voice move into the mainstream. In 2000, Oprah's Angel Network began presenting a $100,000 Use Your Life Award to people who are using their lives to improve the lives of others. She also invested $40 million in the establishment of the Leadership Academy for Girls in South Africa. The 7th-12th-grade school supports the development of a new generation of women leaders who, by virtue of their education, will lead the charge to positively transform themselves, their communities and the larger world around them. We may not all be able to give on that scale, but Oprah is an inspiration for how to be in service.

These community-minded leaders are not alone. In fact, in 2007, two socially conscious businessmen started Executives Without Borders, a New York-based executive matching program that links business volunteers with humanitarian projects in Honduras, Rwanda and India. Jimmy Park, a Harvard Business

School graduate, COO at the media company Cornucopia Arts and former director at the computer software company Radiant Systems, co-founded the group along with Robert Goodwin, a former assistant secretary of the Air Force, who managed logistics at the Pentagon and at the Iraqi Health Ministry before serving as COO of International Aid. Parks described the organization's goal as "the critical link between experienced individuals eager to serve the global community and humanitarian projects around the world."[6] That call to duty really resonated with leaders longing to have an impact outside their companies. The organization now includes 300 executives from companies around the world. Projects include creating software and writing business plans to facilitate sponsorship of Indian girls who would otherwise not be able to attend school, and orchestrating a social media campaign to support medical outreach in Honduras. Executives can work remotely, travel for short-term projects or develop ongoing programs based on their skills, availability and project needs. The win-win-win program helps needed social programs in third-world countries, allows executives to share the skills they have developed over their careers and gives companies a structure for allowing employee giving that brings more meaning to the job.

Letting Go

Changing hats isn't always easy. Remember Ami Bera, the doctor-turned-politician I mentioned in Chapter 6? After he and his wife struggled through medical school to build a comfortable life for themselves and their daughter, he did the unthinkable: he ran for a national office against an established political force. Why would he give up a settled life to invite the scorn, expense and all-consuming pressure of a political campaign? He was surrounded

by those who said he couldn't do it. "It is too difficult," some said.
"You don't have the right background or friends," experienced
political types warned. But Dr. Bera had come to a point in his life
where he couldn't leave the problems to someone else to solve.
"A lot of people are sleep walking, including the leadership," he
says. This brave man decided to be the wake-up call. He ran his
campaign based on stating the obvious: "Things have to change."

Win or lose, Bera considers himself successful if he can make
his opponent pay attention to the important issues. "I am giving
people a chance to talk about the elephant; life is too short to
not discuss the things that are really important." And now, some
of those who advised him against running are among his biggest
supporters.

Bera says the key to taking a chance and giving back in a big
way is letting go of the need to be in charge. "I make a concerted
effort to accept my insignificance," he says. "I can impact and
influence, but I don't control what happens. I can only control
my intentions and how I present myself."

Once you embrace your limitations, it is actually liberating,
Bera maintains. It gives you permission to try despite your
ignorance and flaws. If you do fail, the acknowledgement that
you have the power to improve gives you permission to try again.
"Letting go requires being self-aware," Bera says. "That is a
learned skill and I am still in the process of learning."

On the Offense

So you see, I am by no means alone in my need to change
directions after spending years building my leadership skills and
becoming a vice president at one of the top IT companies in the
world. I'm sure you have had these yearnings too, and I hope one

day you will be able to act on them. For me, I knew it was time to take all that I had learned and focus my energy on activities with a personal purpose. One of those activities is to spread the word about the importance of diversity and authenticity. I retired early from my high-tech career and spent some time decompressing from the intensity of corporate life. Yes, it was difficult to slow down from the breakneck pace that I thrived on for so many years, but I was determined to make the shift. I spent time with my family, traveled, started a nonprofit organization and spent time reflecting on my life. Only then did I begin to envision my life going forward. Although I knew what I wanted to work on, I still took the time to think through how I would approach it.

I am passionate about sharing my message that you can be your unique, authentic self with your own style and be an effective, strong leader. I've walked this path throughout my career and know that it is time to redefine leadership to be more open to all types and styles of people. We have a tendency in organizations to create norms, often unintentionally. It is the nature of people to hire folks like themselves. I carry this message to start the dialogue and effect change throughout all types of organizations — corporate, nonprofit or any type of gathering of people. We need to be conscious of our actions and how we include — and exclude — people. That is the only way we can change the outcome.

I started with the idea of diversity in this book because we must first internalize a belief that any organization is stronger when it is woven with a diverse set of individuals. As I've said several times, diversity has to be more than an HR goal. Bringing together people from different cultures, experiences, preferences, personalities and interests results in a stronger organization that will yield powerful results. I had the unique opportunity to do this while at HP. I saw the power of bringing together all kinds of people from all around the world. It is isn't easy to do, but it is powerful and well worth the conscious effort to thread together a colorful array of talent, cultures and experience into an organization poised to tackle challenges and come to creative solutions.

> *It is powerful and well worth the conscious effort to thread together a colorful array of talent, cultures and experience into an organization poised to tackle challenges and come to creative solutions.*

I end this book with the idea of authenticity because when you embrace diversity in others and value the diversity of yourself, you become a powerful, authentic leader. Being true to yourself is imperative if you want to be a strong leader. How can you lead your organization without having a strong awareness of your own unique talents and perspectives? How can you bring out the best in your team when you are not willing to expose all of yourself? And, lastly, how can you be authentic and not fully understand the power of diversity? Diversity and authenticity go hand in hand. They are the yin and yang of a strong leader. One is the wide array of differences of all people around the world; the other is the full array of uniqueness that makes each individual unlike any other.

As I close this last chapter of the book, I want to share how Jyoti Narula, who I mentioned earlier in this chapter, summarizes the concepts of leadership, diversity and authenticity: "Leadership is about you, your courage, your willingness to walk the path that gives you happiness. Diversity is your willingness to accept an alternate view — not with mind, but with heart. Authenticity is your desire to find yourself amongst the noise and the glitter of the world around you." It all comes back to how you want to show up in this world and what makes you feel fulfilled each and every day.

I have a message to share; it is a message that we are ready to break out of the narrowly defined aspects of what makes a leader and build a more diverse, all-encompassing definition of what makes an extraordinary leader.

I have left the high-tech world of my corporate career, but I have not left my desire to lead in the world. I am leading in my community, my new ventures, and — most importantly — my life. My intention is to inspire people by my words, my actions and my own efforts to make the world a better place. I challenge you to come along with me on this journey and spread the word that it is time to embrace diversity on a whole new level and to be our authentic selves in everything we do, at every moment.

COMMON THREAD

Become part of the fabric of people dedicated to embracing diversity in the world. Join the conversation at www.kimboxinspires.com to stay connected and share your experience and inspiration.

For more information and to book
Kim Box for a speaking engagement,
go to: www.kimboxinspires.com

Or Write to:
Kim Box
8789 Auburn-Folsom Rd. Suite C440
Granite Bay, CA 95746